Dame...

Our c... reminded me the world has se... truly great leaders in it.

Dr Rockwell
9-25-2023

(I look forward to working with you!)

Praise for *The Vagrant*

"A lovely tale of humanity and humility, wrapped in a fast, engaging read. *The Vagrant* will spark leaders of every kind to reflect on who they are."

—Daniel H. Pink, #1 *New York Times* bestselling author of
The Power of Regret, When, and *To Sell Is Human*

"A modern-day fable of self-reflection and transformation, in the spirit of Charles Dickens's *A Christmas Carol* . . . sure to be a lasting favorite not only for fans of leadership but for anyone who loves a great story of fall and redemption."

—David Bach, ten-time *New York Times* bestselling author
of *The Automatic Millionaire* and *The Latte Factor*

"Every leader eventually arrives at a fork in the path. The easy road is seductive but leads to a crash. The tougher road—the road of genuine self-reflection—is the one that leads to lasting impact. *The Vagrant* is an excellent roadmap to that greater path."

—Nido Qubein, president of High Point University

"There is so much insight packed into this little story! The connections, themes, and implications are so subtle and so powerful, I wanted to slow down so I could take it all in—but it pulled me along, like a riptide of revelation, right to its astonishing conclusion. Now I'm reading it a second time . . . and taking notes."

—Dondi Scumaci, author of *Designed for Success:
The 10 Commandments for Women in the Workplace*

"The most dangerous flaw a leader can have is the one they refuse to see. World-renowned leadership authority Dan Rockwell and master storyteller John David Mann bring us a compelling tale of blindness and vision, fall and ultimate redemption—and in the process help us take a really good look at ourselves."

—Bob Burg, author of *Adversaries into Allies* and coauthor of *The Go-Giver*

"*The Vagrant* has everything a great leadership parable needs: believable characters, vivid writing, and a fabulous twist that will stay with you long after you turn the last page."

—Ken Blanchard, coauthor of *The New One Minute Manager®* and *Leading at a Higher Level*

"If you've had your fill of leadership books, take one more step with this one! *The Vagrant* teaches aspects of leadership I haven't seen covered in anything else I've ever read. It will leave you with new questions and powerful insights that will stay with you long after you turn the last page."

—Beverly Kaye, *Wall Street Journal* bestselling author or *Love 'Em or Lose 'Em* and 2022 Industry Legend Award recipient, Institute for Corporate Productivity (i4CP)

"Our opportunity to lead others is predicated on our ability to lead ourselves. This book may be the wake-up call you've needed your entire career."

—Mark Miller, vice president of high performance leadership at Chick-fil-A, Inc. and *Wall Street Journal* bestselling author of *Culture Rules*

"*The Vagrant* takes you on a journey of authenticity that will transform your leadership. If you're ready to do the personal work, the journey starts here."

—Skip Prichard, national bestselling author of *The Book of Mistakes: 9 Secrets to Creating a Successful Future* and CEO of OCLC, Inc.

"A modern-day fable of self-reflection and transformation from two incredible storytellers. Mann and Rockwell will keep you on the edge of your seat from the first page to the last."

—Marshall Goldsmith, *New York Times* #1 bestselling author of
What Got You Here Won't Get You There,
ranked "#1 Leadership Thinker in the World" by Thinkers50

"Leadership starts with the relationship we have with ourselves. *The Vagrant* provides a compelling exploration of one man's powerful journey of self-discovery. An inspiring and meaningful read filled with insights for anyone interested in becoming a more evolved leader."

—Betsy Myers, former executive director of
Center for Public Leadership at
Harvard's Kennedy School of Government
and founding director of Center for Women & Business,
Bentley University

"A compelling story, a surprise ending, and a powerfully valuable lesson along the way. *The Vagrant* is a great book from the dynamic duo of Mann and Rockwell."

—Jon Gordon, ten-time bestselling author of
The Energy Bus and *The Carpenter*

"Spellbinding! Mann and Rockwell have made an invaluable contribution to leadership development in the contemporary world."

—Brandon Webb, founder of SOFREP Media
and former head instructor at
the Naval Special Warfare sniper school

"*The Vagrant* gets to the heart of leadership in a fresh, powerfully engaging way. An inspiring read for any leader aspiring to lift their contribution profile to new heights."

—Douglas R. Conant, *New York Times* bestselling author of
The Blueprint, former CEO of Campbell Soup Company,
and founder and CEO of ConantLeadership

"*The Vagrant* is a fable you'll want to read over and over, that will wake you up to the power of self-awareness. Dan Rockwell and John David Mann make us reflect on who we truly see when we look in the mirror and what may be holding us back. This book will inspire a transformation in all leaders."

—Hubert Joly, senior lecturer at Harvard Business School,
former chairman and CEO of Best Buy and
bestselling author of *The Heart of Business:
Leadership Principles for the Next Era of Capitalism*

"While information is abundant and readily available, true wisdom is scarce and difficult to obtain. *The Vagrant* closes this wisdom gap, revealing that a leader's past does not have to define his future."

—Orin Woodward, *New York Times* bestselling coauthor of
Launching a Leadership Revolution
and an *Inc.* "Top 50 Leadership and Management Expert"

"*The Vagrant* is an irresistible, powerful guide to getting to know yourself. As every entrepreneur knows, business success is all about relationships—and if you don't know yourself, how on earth can anyone else get to know you, like you, and trust you?"

—Rabbi Daniel Lapin,
president of the American Alliance of Jews and Christians
and author of *Thou Shall Prosper:
The Ten Commandments for Making Money*

"*The Vagrant* is a gripping parable that offers a refreshing perspective on leadership and the power of human connection. It inspires us to look beyond the superficial and embrace the complexity of our fellow human beings. I highly recommend this book to anyone looking for a thought-provoking and inspiring read."

—John Ramstead, president of Alpha Principle
and host of the *Eternal Leadership* podcast

Also coauthored by John David Mann

PARABLES

The Go-Giver (with Bob Burg)
The Go-Giver Leader (with Bob Burg)
The Go-Giver Influencer (with Bob Burg)
The Go-Giver Marriage (with Ana Gabriel Mann)
Go-Givers Sell More (with Bob Burg)
A Teacher's Guide to the Go-Giver (with Bob Burg and
Randy Stelter)
The Latte Factor (with David Bach)
Out of the Maze (with Spencer Johnson)
The Recipe (with Chef Charles Carroll)

LEADERSHIP

Take the Lead (with Betsy Myers)
Real Leadership (with John Addison)
The Red Circle (with Brandon Webb)
The Making of a Navy SEAL (with Brandon Webb)

NOVELS

Steel Fear (with Brandon Webb)
Cold Fear (with Brandon Webb)
Blind Fear (with Brandon Webb)

THE
VAGRANT

The Inner Journey
of Leadership

—— **A PARABLE** ——

DAN ROCKWELL

JOHN DAVID MANN

BenBella Books, Inc.
Dallas, TX

BenBella Books, Inc.
10440 N. Central Expressway
Suite 800
Dallas, TX 75231
benbellabooks.com
Send feedback to feedback@benbellabooks.com

BenBella is a federally registered trademark.

Printed in the United States of America
10 9 8 7 6 5 4 3 2 1

Library of Congress Control Number: 2023003570
ISBN 9781637743706 (hardcover)
ISBN 9781637743713 (electronic)

Editing by Gregory Newton Brown
Copyediting by Jennifer Brett Greenstein
Proofreading by Kellie Doherty and Isabelle Rubio
Text design and composition by Jordan Koluch
Cover design by Sarah Avinger
Cover image © Adobe Stock / arkadijschell
Printed by Lake Book Manufacturing

To Dale Marie Rockwell and Ana Gabriel Mann,
our North Stars and the best life companions
either of us could possibly have dreamed of.

"I look back on the way I was then: a young, stupid kid who committed that terrible crime. I want to talk to him. I want to try to talk some sense to him, tell him the way things are. But I can't. That kid's long gone, and this old man is all that's left."

—Red (Morgan Freeman),
in *The Shawshank Redemption*,
written and directed by Frank Darabont,
based on a novella by Stephen King

"Therefore I have uttered what I did not understand, things too wonderful for me, which I did not know."

—the book of Job

"Becoming a leader is synonymous with becoming yourself. It's precisely that simple, and it's also that difficult."

—Warren Bennis, *On Becoming a Leader*

vagrant | vāgrənt | noun: In ornithology, a bird that has strayed or been blown off its usual range or migratory route.

—*New Oxford American Dictionary*

Contents

1. THE VAGRANT

You know how they say, "I wouldn't know that guy if I tripped over him?" Well, I actually tripped over him—walked right into his outstretched legs before I'd noticed anyone sitting there. And even then, I didn't recognize him. I should have, but I didn't. At least not yet.

I still wonder how things would have turned out if I had.

The day started out so well. Everything was going my way.

It was the last Thursday in April. I had been at

Mercy Hospital for going on three years. Three excellent, auspicious, turbocharged years.

When I arrived the place was a mess. Riddled with inefficiencies, rife with redundancies, shackled by a dozen incompatible information systems that couldn't talk to each other. I already had something of a reputation as a guy who could get things done, and I was determined to keep earning that reputation.

"Whatever it takes!" That was my rallying cry.

It took me a full year just to chase down where all the biggest problem areas were, another to work out the solutions. Year three, which we were in the process of wrapping up, was for implementation: a hodgepodge of competing legacy systems, streamlined and compressed like layers of deli meat, integrated together and smashed inside a simple, friendly hoagie roll of a user interface. I dubbed it "the Hero Project," both because of its structural resemblance to a sandwich and because it would allow our doctors to get their noses out of those old byzantine chart-keeping systems and focus on actually being doctors.

By this time, I was co-leading a department of forty employees, running everything from the help desk to software development and deployment in every ward and unit. Had an excellent relationship with my boss, Norman, the CIO.

I was on my way to the top.

So it was no surprise, that sunny spring morning, when I was called up to the seventh floor. I'd been looking forward to the promotion for weeks.

Except that what happened when I got there was very much a surprise.

Biggest surprise of my life, in fact.

And thirty minutes later I was back down on the third floor, walking out of my office—no longer *my* office—carrying a file box with my personal effects. I hadn't been promoted after all. That wasn't why I'd been called up to the seventh floor. Quite the opposite.

I'd been *fired*.

Making that thirty-foot slog to the elevator was like drifting through a nightmare I couldn't wake up from no matter how hard I tried.

I'd never been fired from anything in my life. Something was very, very wrong with this picture.

It never occurred to me that the problem might be me.

I took a side door out of the building to avoid being seen. Heading around a back corner toward the entrance to the underground garage, I didn't notice the homeless guy sitting there, back to the wall, legs jutting out like sticks of driftwood.

He wore a dirty green wool hat and one of those orange DayGlo construction vests, though most of the Glo was long gone. Gloves with the fingers cut off. How old was he? Impossible to say. Fifties, maybe?

Or maybe he was only a few years older than me, just in terrible shape.

In any case, these observations did not come until a few moments later, because, as I said, at first I didn't even see him.

I tripped, took a tumble.

My box went sprawling, all my possessions spilling out over the asphalt.

"Oh, for cryin' out loud!" I yelled at him. "If you have to panhandle, go do it around the front of the building!"

Which was a ridiculous thing to say, of course. There was no panhandling allowed out in front of Mercy Hospital. It was only later that it occurred to me, he probably wasn't even panhandling at all.

"Tripped . . . o'er yourself," he slurred.

Obviously the man was drunk, or out of his mind. Probably both.

"Actually, I tripped over *you*," I muttered as I picked myself up and moved to collect my scattered things. "Which I wouldn't have, if you weren't sitting out here in the middle of the walkway!"

"You got . . . you got . . ." He was having a hard time getting out complete sentences. "Got in your way . . ."

"Me? *I* got in my way? WHAT IS WRONG WITH YOU, MAN?"

A few people stared at me as they walked by on their way to the garage. All at once, I realized how foolish I must look. There I was, my stuff scattered all over the asphalt, shouting at this poor bum.

I couldn't remember ever having felt so humiliated.

". . . impediments . . ." he mumbled.

"What?"

"Impediments . . . of the apocalypse they . . . fly on wings of . . . gold, but it's . . . an illusion . . ."

He broke off into a coughing spell, hacking so badly I thought he was going to heave up his lungs, but he kept on trying to talk. I barely caught the words: "volume . . . age . . ." and a third that sounded like "Sufism."

Great, just great. A religious nut.

He held up one finger as he coughed, signaling me to hang on.

I waited. Why, I couldn't have told you, but I stood waiting for him to finish saying whatever it was he had to say.

Finally the coughing subsided, and after a few wheezing breaths he got out one more word: "Cer'nty."

And with that, he slumped back against the building, as if fully spent from the effort.

Volume . . . age . . . Sufism . . . certainty.

Impediments of the apocalypse.

Uh-huh.

Oh well, I told myself. *At least he isn't dangerous.*

How wrong I was.

I finished gathering up my things, stuffed them back into the box, and headed below into the parking garage.

On the way, I started feeling bad about having yelled at the man. It wasn't his fault he was a derelict. Or you know what, maybe it was his fault, but I still felt bad for losing my cool at him.

Once I'd got my box into the car, safely stashed on the floor of the front passenger seat, I locked up again and hiked back out of the garage and around to the pavement.

He wasn't there.

It took a few minutes, but I finally located him out behind the building, reclining in the shade of a dumpster.

"Hey, man," I said. "Sorry I kind of . . ." Feeling suddenly awkward, I wasn't sure how to end the sentence, so instead I reached into my pocket, pulled out my billfold, peeled off a spanking new twenty, and handed it to him.

He made no move toward the bill.

"Take it," I insisted.

He reached out and took the bill, looking up at me as he did so—and that was when I got my first and only good look at the man's face. There was something familiar about him, but I couldn't quite place it. In fact, I was about to ask his name, inquire whether I knew him from somewhere, when he took me by surprise.

He handed me back the twenty!

"You need this more than I do," he croaked.

To be honest, I was speechless. "Fine, then," I said, and I snatched back the bill. I didn't feel great about it, but I jammed the twenty in my pocket, turned, and walked away.

In my defense, I was still reeling from the ten-ton catastrophe that had just been dropped on me, up on the seventh floor.

Now *that* was an apocalypse, all right.

Had to give the homeless guy credit, he was certainly right about that one.

I trekked back into the murk of the parking garage to climb into my car and take a moment alone to think. At my parking spot, I stopped.

The car was gone.

2. THE FILE BOX

Maybe you've heard this one.

State cop pulls off the freeway at the scene of a crash. Trucker sideswiped a Beamer. Car is totaled, lying on its side thirty feet off the road. Cop gets out of his Dodge Charger, walks over to where the driver sits on the ground rocking back and forth, moaning. The guy was miraculously thrown clear, but his left arm is gone, nothing left but a bloody stump. He must have had it propped out the driver's-side window.

As the cop gets closer, he can make out what the guy is saying.

"My BMW ... my BMW ...!"

Cop says, "Sir, I was you, I'd be less upset about

the car and more concerned about the fact that my left arm's gone missing."

The guy whips his head up at the cop, eyes wild, and goes, "*What?*" He looks down at the stump where his left arm used to be and screams, "MY ROLEX!"

Ha-ha.

In my case it wasn't a BMW; it was a Toyota SW20 MR2, what they call "the poor man's Ferrari." I called it my *racecar*. In prime shape, too, with just two months left on the lease. But it wasn't the missing car that delivered the gut punch that had me reeling, and it certainly wasn't a Rolex—pretentious things, if you ask me.

It was my file box.

The car was gone, which meant my file box was gone.

Which meant everything *in* my file box was gone.

I slumped down in a heap, my back to the dank concrete wall, and so help me, I started to cry.

Let me tell you about what was in that box.

A few books. *Patton on Leadership. The Art of War. You Can Negotiate Anything.* All heavily dog-eared and sticky-noted. Those I could replace.

A family photo. Me, Sis, Mom, and Dad, the last time the four of us were all together. I was pretty sure it was the only copy in existence.

My MBA degree, signed by my favorite professor, now deceased.

A few framed awards and two trophies, the first featuring a little brass-plated figure in the process of throwing a long pass. High school state championship: quarterback, captain of the team. I was proud of that one—but even prouder of the other award, from my first place of employment, fresh out of grad school: a five-pointed brass star mounted upright on an acrylic base over the inscription "Rising Star," with a second inscription underneath in smaller type that read, "Presented to Bob Barab in Recognition of His Outstanding Leadership."

And finally, my high school yearbook, page 102 of which sported a photo of me, grinning, over a scrawled inscription from the principal: "To a Born Leader: Make Us Proud!"

Which was exactly what I thought I was doing—at least until that morning.

The police station was only a few blocks away. I walked. Filled out the report. Got the expected cop spiel. "Don't worry, Mr. Barab, we'll find your car." That's what he said with his mouth. His eyes said, *Fat chance.*

I cabbed it to my apartment. Barely bigger than a postage stamp, it was all I could afford in that chichi neighborhood, but it was a homey little place, and I'd put a lot of care into it.

I poured myself a tumbler of something expensive. Stood there in my little kitchen, swirling the squat little glass and listening to the ice cubes go *clink-clink*. Then poured it all out into the sink. Drowning my sorrows in a pool of overpriced Scotch . . . it was too cliché to bear.

Besides, I was already feeling foggy enough.

I rinsed out the glass, refilled it with ice water, then dropped into my favorite overstuffed leather chair and tried to sort out my situation.

My racecar. Gone.

That file box with my most prized possessions. Gone.

And my job, too?

What?

How could I possibly be *fired*? Where had *that* come from? To be honest, reviewing the entire forty-person department in my mind, I'd have thought I was the least likely employee to be deemed dispensable. This wasn't just out of the blue. This was from the farthest reaches of outer space.

I set the glass down and lurched out of my chair to walk a few circles in my little living room as I replayed the scene.

"I'm doing you a favor here, Bob," my boss had had the gall to say.

Oh, really? How was letting me go without warning, without even giving a good reason, or any reason at all, a *favor*?

"If we were terminating with cause," he'd explained when I posed the question, "you'd have to forego severance. I was the one who lobbied for termination *without* cause."

I understood the distinction. The expression "termination without cause" was misleading; all it meant was that the employee hadn't done anything wrong. Budget issues, operational restructuring, department-wide downsizing . . . there could be any number of employer pressures behind a dismissal that had nothing to do with the employee.

"*With* cause," on the other hand, would have meant I'd brought this on myself through poor performance, or because of some policy or ethics violation.

Which, according to Norman, had actually been on the table—someone, some unnamed hospital officer, had wanted me fired for cause!

And honestly, that tripped all my circuit breakers.

Cause? What "cause" could there possibly be? For heaven's sake, I'd *saved* that department!

"You know what, Bob?" he'd said, his voice steady

as a suspended guillotine blade. "It's really better you don't ask. You had a good run, all right? The project's finished. Let's just leave it at that."

A *good run?*

As I paced my living room, I slipped one hand into my pants pocket and came out with that twenty, the one I had tried to give the homeless guy. I held it out in front of me with thumb and forefinger, then stuck it up on my faux mantelpiece and stared at it, thinking about the man's sorry condition and senseless rant.

Volume . . . age . . . Sufism . . . certainty. Impediments of the apocalypse.

I shook my head. "How does a guy turn out like that?" I said out loud.

It never entered my mind, not for one moment, that I might want to ask that same question about myself.

3. BARGAINING

I awoke the next morning alert, refreshed, and with a clear sense of conviction, as if my brain had been power-washed of all the previous day's fog.

It had all been one big misunderstanding! Some gigantic, weird tangle of garbled information—just like everything at Mercy when I'd first arrived. All I had to do was get to the bottom of the tangle. Isolate the issue. Identify the so-called "cause" and whatever silly accusation lay behind it. Clear up the confusion. Norman was a reasonable guy. Not the brightest light bulb on the Christmas tree, but reasonable.

I needed to talk with my boss.

I cabbed it to a nearby rental place, picked out a Civic (always my ride of choice, prior to the racecar), and drove straight over to Mercy. I half expected to see the homeless guy again when I pulled into the back lot, but he was nowhere in evidence.

Janice, the lobby receptionist, looked startled to see me. She greeted me with a confused, worried smile. "Morning . . . Bob?"

I nodded a greeting and strode past, headed for the elevator, took it straight to the seventh floor.

Where they wouldn't let me in to see Norman.

Back down to the lobby, back over to Janice's reception desk.

I smiled.

"Janice," I said. "Can you get me Norman on the phone?"

She looked at me for a long beat, then said in a low voice, "Bob, you shouldn't be here."

I leaned in, aftershave close, and spoke softly. "Janice. Please."

After another extended beat she relented, looking none too happy about it. She pressed a few buttons and spoke into her headset. "Hi Dana, Janice at reception. Is Norman available for a moment?"

She handed me a handset and pushed another button. We waited for twenty seconds, Janice and I. Then a voice came over my handset, rough from the weight of bourbon and responsibility.

"Davison."

I took a breath.

"Norman. Bob Barab here. Listen—"

"Bob, this is completely inappropriate. You need to hang up now."

"Please, Norman, just hear me out, just for—"

"Barab." He shot my name like throwing the bolt on a prison door. "Don't make me get the board of directors involved."

Board of directors?!

Before I could even think of a response to that one, he added two more words: "Or worse."

And cut the line.

I handed the dead handset back to Janice.

Or worse?

What was worse than involving the hospital's entire board of directors?

I retreated outside to my rental, where I pulled out my cell phone, slumped down in my seat, and called in. "Hello," I said, carefully disguising my voice. "Can I speak with a David Jayne? On the third floor, I believe?"

I heard a sigh on the other end. "Bob," said Janice. "You should leave."

"I did leave, Janice. Do you see me there?" Silence. "Just put me through to David, Janice. There's got to be at least one human being in there who'll talk to me."

She sighed again, then said, "Please hold."

I waited a moment, then heard the crisp tenor of the young man who'd been my right hand for the past thirty-three months.

"Cynthia Sharpe's office, David Jayne speaking."

Cynthia Sharpe's office?

He was working for *Cynthia* now?

"Wow," I said. "That was fast."

I heard the hiss of an exhale. "Bob. Oh, man . . ." His voice had dropped a few decibels. Obviously, he didn't want to be overheard. "How are you doing? My God. How are you handling . . . everything?"

"Tell you the truth, David, I don't even know what 'everything' is. Have you heard anything? Anything at all? About, you know . . . *why?*"

"Not a word. Not a whisper. I was totally freaked out when I heard. And you don't have any idea? I mean, what did *he* say?"

Norman, he meant.

"Terminated without cause." I wasn't about to repeat what Norman had said about the possibility of there actually *being* a cause, not even to David. "Not a clue why. Right out of the wild blue yonder."

"Oh, man," he repeated. "I hate this, Bob. Hate it." David sounded as upset as I felt. "It feels so incredibly . . . *creepy*. When I heard what went down, and that they were moving me across the hall to Cynthia's office, I thought about quitting on the spot, right then and there. Thought about it hard. Shoot, hang on—" I heard his hand cover the mouthpiece and the muffled *mwah mwah mwah* of a background conversation. Then he was back, his voice practically a whisper. "Between you and me, I'm still thinking about it."

"No—no way," I said. "You've got to stay. None of this has anything to do with you."

"Yeah, but working for *Cynthia*? And after what they did to you? I feel like a traitor just sitting at this desk."

"Hey, don't talk like that. What'd I teach you?"

I heard him sigh. "Whatever it takes."

"You better believe it," I said. "*Whatever* it takes. You have to do what you have to do. Don't worry about me. You know me, I'll land on my feet."

Though I confess, I was secretly a little thrilled to hear he'd thought about quitting.

"Listen," said David, even more quietly now. I had to press the phone to my ear to make out the words. "If you land some cherry position at another firm?

And you need an executive assistant? Don't forget your man Friday. I'd give notice here in a heartbeat. Half a heartbeat."

So help me, I nearly teared up. "You got it."

Touched as I was by David's loyalty, the warm fuzzy glow was gone by the time I'd hit the END CALL button.

Cynthia Sharpe.

Cynthia freaking Sharpe.

I'd always liked Cynthia. She was so darn smart. You could always count on a conversation with Cynthia being an entertaining and challenging experience.

Yet I never really trusted her. Something about her always rubbed me the wrong way. "She could cut you on Friday and you wouldn't realize you were bleeding till Monday." That was the word on Cynthia. Ambitious. Ruthless.

You can't say "Cynthia" without the "sin."

The moment I'd heard David's unhappy whispers, I'd understood what had happened. That "cause" Norman had so vaguely alluded to had to have come from somewhere, and I was pretty sure I knew where.

Somehow, Cynthia had sabotaged me. I didn't know how, but she'd turned Norman against me. I was sure of it.

I drove halfway down the block, pulled into a parking place, and waited. It was a few hours till lunchtime, but right now I had nowhere else to be.

The Bitter Brew. Coffee and sandwiches in the daytime, craft beer in the evenings.

I sat in my car, stewing.

Sure enough, a few hours later, there she came, down the sidewalk past my rented Civic. She opened the door to the Bitter Brew and stepped inside.

I waited another few minutes—long enough for her to place her order and take her coffee to her usual table—then went in. I walked straight over and took the seat facing her.

She didn't even blink.

Cynthia never blinked.

I said nothing, just lifted my hands and began a slow clap as I stared at her.

"Well," she purred. "Look what the dog dragged in."

"Nicely done, Cynthia."

"Yeah? And exactly what did I do, Bob?"

"I don't know—but I know you did something."

"Hope I enjoyed it."

I leaned all the way across her table and hissed in her face, "You won't get away with this."

She looked at me with her almond-shaped Cynthia eyes. If she'd had a tail, it would have given one little twitch, nothing more.

"Go home, Bob."

I know, I know. The five stages of grief. I get it. Got it then, even as it was happening. But hear me out.

Yes, I woke up that morning in denial. ("Hey, it was all a misunderstanding!" Seriously, Bob?) And by lunchtime I was lashing out at Cynthia. Anger. Second stage. I get it. And I knew what supposedly came next: bargaining.

Thank you very much, Dr. Kübler-Ross.

Except, wasn't bargaining exactly what was called for here? Haggling with fate, negotiating with circumstance, whatever you want to call it, this whole situation smacked of craziness, made no sense whatsoever—and some sense of the whole thing was what I desperately needed to make.

Unable to come up with a good parting shot after Cynthia's "Go home, Bob," I climbed back into my rented Civic and went home.

And spent the weekend thinking it through.

I considered legal action, but Norman had made it clear that the powers that be at Mercy were not happy with me and were more than prepared to litigate if it came to that. And that it wouldn't end well for me if they did. I didn't think he was bluffing. I needed to find some other course of action, something more effective than a frontal attack.

By Sunday afternoon, I'd come up with a plan. The more I thought about it, the more I liked it. It would take a little patience and a little work. I could do that.

First things first.

I had eight weeks' severance coming, but that would be gone in a wink. My sense of dignity resisted going on unemployment, and even if I did, it wouldn't last forever. And I wasn't about to touch my savings. I needed a job.

And not just any job—the right job.

A job that would not only tide me over financially but also provide the perfect springboard for step two. Call it victory, call it revenge.

I called it *doing whatever it takes*.

There were two other competing hospitals in town. I'd go secure a position at one or the other. Burnish my reputation for problem-solving to a gleam. Advance a notch or two on the salary scale. Gain some yards on the gridiron. Then get my old job at Mercy back—at a significantly higher rate of pay.

Have a little patience. Put in the work.

Whatever it takes.

And before you could say "Quarterback sneak!" things would all be going my way again.

4. MR. VOLUME

It took no more than five phone calls to line up the two interviews. Data systems expertise like mine was a precious commodity in this town, especially when combined with real-world experience in the maddeningly complicated field of health care. I was pretty sure both places would jump at the chance to scoop me up.

The first interview went as smooth as twelve-year-old single malt Scotch. Norman had had the decency to give me a reasonably good letter of recommendation, and my résumé (which did not detail the reason for my departure from Mercy) was golden.

"Your qualifications are impressive," the man said, leafing through my CV one more time. He nodded and looked up at me. "Anyone would be lucky to have you on board."

I smiled. Was that a bidding war I sensed in the offing?

The second interview went even better than the first. I left the building a happy man.

Happy, and relieved. How long would I need to work there before Mercy came back with an offer? Not long.

Or hey, maybe I'd like it so much, I'd stay.

All the next day, I kept myself busy around the apartment. Making a fresh batch of pasta. Doing bills. Vacuuming. Trying not to be that guy sitting by the phone, although I knew very well that's exactly who I was.

It was late Friday morning when I got the first call. It was thumbs-down.

"I wish we could open up a position," the man said. "I pushed and pushed, but no joy. I hate to see you go to the competition, but they'll be well served."

The second call came that afternoon—and it was practically a replay of the first.

Wow, I thought. I did not see that coming.

Okay. Plan B.

Have a little patience. Put in the work.

Whatever it takes.

On Monday morning I started making more calls. By the end of Tuesday I had half a dozen meetings lined up all over town. Not in the health care industry, but they were all information management positions that demanded a similar level of expertise. Out of six appointments, I figured I'd get at least four solid offers, then weigh the various factors carefully before taking my pick of the lot.

The interviews all went well, but there was some subtext going on I couldn't quite figure out. The first guy seemed a little . . . cool. Wouldn't quite look me in the eye. I thought nothing of it, but then the second guy gave me a similar feeling.

And one by one, the answers came back, like a series of firecracker fuses that all fizzled before reaching the *pop*. Sorry. Board wouldn't budge. Couldn't quite justify the salary. We're going another way.

Okay . . . plan C.

Have a little patience.

Put in the work.

Who was it who said, "There is no shame in a tactical retreat," Sun Tzu or George Patton? I looked it up online; it was Jean-Luc Picard.

The following week I went on a round of interviews at lesser companies—all decent management positions but well beneath my pay level and experience. None

would be enough to keep me in my current apartment
for long without having to start dipping into my savings. But I had to do *something*.

And again, things got weird.

The last HR guy I met with concluded what I had
thought was a strong interview with this little hand gre-
nade: "Frankly speaking, Bob, you're overqualified for
anything we might have open here. We just wouldn't
be able to meet the pay scale you're accustomed to."

So I pressed him on that. I hated to do it, and did
my best not to have it come out like groveling, but I
needed to know: What pay scale did he think they
could meet?

He looked down at his desk and fiddled with a pen.
"Well," he said, "frankly, we're looking for someone
who's . . . more of a fit with our culture."

A fit with their culture?

I sat in the parking lot in my rented Civic, wearing
the same look on my face that I'd seen in newscasts of
stricken town residents in the aftermath of catastrophic
tornadoes.

A look that said, *What just happened here?*

Hey, Dr. Kübler-Ross—where does "bafflement"
fit into those stages of grief?

I pulled out my phone and put in a call to Gavin.

Gavin was a colleague. Correction: former

colleague. A brilliant tech guy who stayed completely out of office politics and was a key player in our project. We didn't know each other well; I'd never say so out loud, but I'd always seen him as kind of a dweeb. I knew he was a straight shooter, though, and if I wanted an objective outsider's take on personnel dynamics, I figured Gavin was the one to ask.

I knew Gavin would answer his cell anytime, day or night.

Sure enough, he picked up on the first ring.

I told him about that last interview and the HR guy's "more of a fit with our culture" remark. "Do you have any idea what he's talking about, Gav? Have I got some sort of bad rap on the street that I don't know about?"

Gavin gave it to me straight.

"Sure," he said. "I get what he's saying. You're *loud*."

"I'm *loud*? What are you talking about?"

"You don't listen. You talk. When you walk into a room, you suck up all the oxygen. There's nothing left for the rest of us to breathe. I've seen meetings where, when you leave the room, everyone takes a big breath, because once you're gone, there's finally enough air to go around."

He went silent. I struggled to absorb all that, but honestly, I was having trouble getting past that word.

Loud?

I've known guys who shout. You know the ones I'm talking about: you see them at airport boarding gates, the self-important wheeler-dealers barking into their cell phones at ninety decibels. I am not that guy.

"What do you mean, *loud*?" I said.

"Sorry, man, but . . . you're loud. Even when you aren't saying anything, you're loud. You take up space. I'm sure you don't mean to. I'm sure it's not personal. But you fill the room. You're like a giant gas balloon. When someone else tries to talk, you up the volume. You *fill* the volume. You are Mr. Volume."

I was speechless.

Mr. Volume?

For days after that call with Gavin, the phrase nagged at me like a pebble in my shoe, though I didn't quite know why.

I should have, but I didn't.

At least not yet.

5. A FALL FROM GRACE

Maybe I've mentioned this already: I like nice things. I'm not a snob about it, but I've never apologized for it, either. I've worked hard for the things I enjoy. My racecar. My apartment. My pasta maker.

My clothes.

They say clothes make the man. Not true, of course, but they do *express* the man, and I've always had a fondness for fine threads. It's not vanity. I'm not trying to impress anyone.

As I said: I just like nice things.

I'd been buying my suits and jackets at Jonathan's Trading Company for years. Also my shirts, socks, even belts and shoes. I always looked forward to a Jonathan's visit. The smell of good Italian wool, the hushed ambience. The care the staff took in fitting and tailoring. They made you feel like they were decking you out for a coronation. Understated elegance, all the way.

Turns out, it's a totally different experience when you work there as an employee.

Facing the fact that more ideal opportunities were closed off to me for the time being (although I was still baffled as to why), I decided to look for management positions in smaller companies. Nothing.

Then I tried even smaller companies. Local outfits that might need a data-management pro to help streamline their systems. Startups.

Nothing.

Finally, after five interminable weeks, I applied for a job as a retail clerk at Jonathan's.

You read that right. In less than two months I went from running a forty-person department at a major metropolitan hospital to a job in retail, helping other men pick out power ties.

Talk about a fall from grace.

And the work wasn't easy, mainly because of how demanding the customers could be. I soon learned just how much abuse these clerks took—and how much they heaped on each other.

Especially on the new guy.

For example: Most of Jonathan's customers were regulars, and some were known for being more difficult than others. When the worst customers walked in the door, the other clerks always found ingenious ways to ensure that I would be the one waiting on them.

They also devised creative ways to hog double spaces in the store's minuscule parking lot out back, thereby forcing me to park my rented Civic on the street, where I had to feed the meter all day long, which added insult to injury by being both awkward and expensive. If I left my lunch in the staff fridge in the morning, I could be sure it would be gone before I had the chance to eat it.

Stupid, puerile behavior, grade-school stuff, but it made a misery of my days. It was not difficult to tell how much the other salespeople disliked me.

I'd be lying if I said the feeling wasn't mutual.

And I had not quite anticipated just how *humiliating* the whole experience would be. I'd always been a *client* at this store, and now here I was, fitting people's pants, brushing off their jackets, telling them how good they looked (whether true or not). I did everything I could to hide from any customers who knew me.

For a while, I succeeded.

It was nearly three weeks into my sentence at Jonathan's when Mercy's own Larch Desmond strode in to pick up a trio of suits. Anesthesiologist, handsome as sin, God's gift to women: a legend in his own mind. Dr. Larch Desmond was so vain, so lacking in self-awareness, we used to call him "Norma" behind his back after the narcissistic, washed-up screen star from *Sunset Boulevard.*

I prayed he wouldn't recognize me. There was no reason for him to; I wasn't waiting on him. He had a clerk he'd worked with for years, an older guy who fawned all over him.

Yet sure enough, as Larch stood at the register, waiting while his Amex went through the card reader, he glanced over—and who should he see but good ol' Bob.

"Barab!" he exclaimed. "Son of a gun! I heard you were here." He turned to his obsequious suit caddy. "Barab used to work over at Mercy. Sharp guy, destined for great things, till he screwed up." He leaned in and continued in a stage whisper that could be heard back in the fitting rooms.

"Scuttlebutt is, Bob was angling for the boss's job. Boom! Out the door! Damn shame, if you ask—"

I lost it.

"Get out!" I said. "Get out of here, Desmond! Take your Amex Gold Card, your cheap hair plugs and fake tan, *and get out of my store!*"

You could see him go pale beneath the tan. He snatched up his charge card and parcels and hit the bricks.

I turned to find myself facing the store manager. By the look on his face, I guessed he wasn't too happy with me right at that moment.

And just like that, for the second time in as many months, I was fired.

You've probably already guessed what it was that so provoked me that day at Jonathan's: there was a kernel of truth to Larch's blather.

Had I thought about Norman's job? I had. To be honest, I believed I would have been pretty good at it. An improvement over Norman, anyway.

But had I ever breathed a word of those thoughts? To anyone?

Of course not.

Just to make sure I wasn't crazy, I called David from the parking lot and asked him if he'd heard anything about the rumor Larch had reported. Not a peep, he said, adding, "Consider the source." He had a point there: Larch Desmond was not exactly the most trust-worthy guy.

Part of me wanted to ask David if he'd ever heard anything like Gavin's "Mr. Volume" crack from anyone on the team, but I held my tongue. Maybe I was afraid to hear the answer.

I thanked David and clicked off.

And sat in my rented Civic, brooding.

David's assurances notwithstanding, Larch must have heard *something*. He might be malicious enough to invent such a thing just to torture me, but I didn't think he had the imagination.

Had I really been that indiscreet?

Was that what got me fired?

I thought back over the months and years I'd been there.

No, I was quite sure I hadn't said or done anything in Norman's presence that would have betrayed those hidden ambitions. Nor had I said anything to anyone else, as far as I could remember.

Still, after what Gavin said, I was starting to doubt my own judgment.

I won't lie: the whole thing shook me up pretty bad.

I couldn't find a decent job, or even a semidecent one. I'd just been canned from a bare-subsistence gig in retail. Time—which is to say, my bank account—was running out. If I wanted to hang on to my place, I might have to think at some point about raiding my savings. Even then, I couldn't go without work forever.

And I had to admit, I was still smarting from the sheer humiliation of that spectacle I'd made of myself at Jonathan's.

I needed a hug. Or a drink. Or maybe a frontal lobotomy.

No, what I needed was a friendly face.

So I went to see Lacy.

6. LACY

Lacy worked as an ER nurse at Mercy. Not that we ever bumped into each other there; the ER was a world away from the third floor and the whole admin wing.

Lacy had a kind heart and a tomboy laugh. If there was ever a natural-born caregiver, Lacy was it. We'd been an item for a while, early in my tenure at Mercy, but I broke it off after five or six months when I couldn't see it going anywhere serious. We still saw each other, though, every now and then, just as friends.

When I called to suggest we meet for dinner, she told me she was working the graveyard shift that night, so I offered to pick her up when she got off work the next morning and take her out to breakfast, then drop her back at her car.

"I'll pull up right at the E room entrance at eight," I said.

"Have you ever even seen the ER, Bob? The place where actual patients go?"

"Ha-ha. Hey, go easy on me, okay?"

"Rough week?" she said.

"Rough month. I'll tell you all about it over omelets."

The next morning I did exactly that. I told her about being fired from Mercy, the theft of my car and possessions, and the humiliating string of fruitless interviews. I left out the conversation with Gavin and the episode at Jonathan's; recounting as much as I did was already painful enough. A man can take only so much unburdening of the soul at one time.

Lacy was as mortified as I knew she would be.

"Ohmigosh, that's awful! Bob, you need someone you can talk to—more than me, I mean. A shoulder you can cry on. Are you seeing anyone?"

"Actually, I'm sort of in between relationships right now," I said.

She laughed.

"What's so funny about that?"

"Bob," she said. "How can you be 'between'

relationships when you've never really been *in* a relationship?"

"Oh, that's cold, Lacy. That's really cold. And it's not true. We had a good thing going for a while there."

"You had a good thing going, maybe, I don't really know. Me, I was just a guilty bystander."

I didn't reply to that one. I knew she was kidding around with me, but I was not in a kidding mood. I suppose you could say I sulked.

"Oh, c'mon." She reached over and poked my arm. "You have no sense of humor."

Now that stung.

"What are you talking about? My jokes are legendary." I was serious. I had always thought of myself as a pretty funny guy.

"I'm not talking about jokes," she said. "Having a sense of humor isn't about clever punch lines. It's about having a sense of perspective. Like, seeing the irony of a situation."

"Okay, how's this for perspective?" I said. "I'm baring my woes here, telling you about how I've lost—" I ticked the items off on my fingers "—my job, my car, and oh, I don't know, my professional reputation, maybe my *career*, and you're telling me about my character flaws? I think *that's* pretty ironic."

"That's not perspective, Bob, that's just self-pity."

We ate in silence for a moment. Then I said, "They threw me out, Lace. Like a used Kleenex. Without even giving me a reason. Don't I have a right to be angry?"

She reached across the table and put her hand on top of mine. "Of course you do. But you don't just get angry. You spill your anger all over everyone else. Flail at it like a blindfolded kid swinging at a birthday party piñata. Only when you make contact, it's not perspective that tumbles out but just more of your issues."

"What are you saying, I shouldn't talk about it? I should just swallow it all?"

"Of course you should talk about it. That's why I'm here, right? But you don't talk, Bob. You *rage*."

I *rage*?

"That's not true!" I protested. "I do not 'rage.' No more than anyone else, I mean."

"Really," she said. She looked pensive for a moment, then put down her utensils and looked me in the eyes.

"Bob, what do you think happened here?"

"Here?"

"Us."

"Us," I repeated. "You mean, the breakup?"

She gave a little shrug. *Well?*

"Um, how do I put this diplomatically," I said. "I was under the impression that breaking it off was on *my* initiative?"

"Oh, Bob," she said softly, and she gave me a look like I was a lost kitten.

And all at once I saw something I'd never seen before.

The breakup had been her idea. Not mine. She'd just been too kindhearted to ever press the point.

The ride back to Mercy was silent. Lacy may have said a few things I barely heard—Was I okay? She was sure things would turn out for me; was there anything she could do?—and I may have even come back with some empty answers.

But the drive still felt like silence.

After dropping her off with some vague assurance that I was fine, not to worry, I turned my rented Civic around and headed back to my apartment.

I couldn't stop thinking about our relationship, rewinding the months of footage in my head, looking at every scene, every moment, in the light of this new information. It was like a movie I thought I'd seen when it was first released in the theater, but now that I was watching it on TV, I didn't recognize any of it.

It was *she* who broke it off?

I stopped at a red light and put my hand to the ache in my chest. I couldn't breathe. Was I having some kind of cardiac event? Perfect, Bob—a heart attack at a red light.

I pushed out a big shuddering exhale, then lifted my hand and touched two fingers to my cheek. It was wet.

Tears?

And it hit me like a thunderclap. I wasn't having a heart attack. It was worse than having a heart attack.

I was heartbroken.

More than that, I was . . . *lonely.*

I became aware of the car behind me honking. The light had turned. I gave a wave and drove on, the movie in my head now replaced with that single disorienting thought.

I was *lonely.*

And, honestly, I didn't know what to do with that.

I didn't think I'd ever felt lonely in my life.

7. VANITY OF VANITIES

It was a cool June day out, perfect for walking, and I needed to clear my head, or try to anyway. Two months had passed since I'd been *fired* (I still couldn't wrap my brain around that word), and my quest for answers was going nowhere fast. The conversation with Lacy had left me only more confused than ever.

After parking my rented Civic back at my apartment building, I went for a stroll in a nearby park. On the way, I passed by Merl, sitting on his bench, feeding the pigeons.

Merlin was a park fixture whose mission in life seemed to be handing out little slips of paper with Bible verse numbers printed on them. Just the number, not the actual verse. I think the idea was that we were supposed to go look it up ourselves. No one knew if "Merlin" was his real name or just something he'd picked out at some point in his unknown past. I didn't think I'd ever heard him speak a word.

Merl was a little crazy—okay, probably a lot crazy—but harmless. Just your garden-variety street-corner evangelist. Doesn't every city have a Merl or two?

"What's the good word, Merl?" I said as I approached.

This was what I always said when our paths crossed, because that was Merl's thing: handing out the Good Word.

Literally, one word.

On the back of each tract he handed out, Merl would always scribble a single word, selected on the spur of the moment, apparently chosen specifically for that particular person, according to criteria unknown to anyone but Merl. It might be SMILE or JOY, GLADNESS or PEACE, RADIANCE or BROTHERHOOD, but it was always some variation on the theme of Merl's unflaggingly sunny disposition.

I would take the slip of paper, stuff it in my pocket, and wait till later to throw it away. It didn't feel right to toss it in the trash right in front of the guy.

So it was a well-established routine when I said, as always, "What's the good word, Merl?"

He put up one finger, bidding me to wait.

After a little hunting through his sheaf of paper strips, he carefully pulled one out, then scribbled on the back of it with his felt-tip pen and handed it to me, beaming with accomplishment, like he'd just pulled me out of a burning building.

"Ecclesiastes 1:2," said the print on the front.

I knew that one; it was one of Merl's favorites. *Vanity of vanities, saith the preacher, vanity of vanities. All is vanity.*

I turned the slip over and was mildly surprised.

Normally Merl just handwrote a single word, nothing else—but today he'd gone the extra mile and taken a moment to add the date and my name. Why, I had no idea. Maybe he did it in case my slip of paper got lost, like your mom stitching your name into your underwear for summer camp? Who knew? There was no point in trying to follow Merl's logic.

"Thanks, Merl." I slid the thing into my pocket and walked on, shaking my head over Merl's word of the day and what an incredibly unfortunate choice it was:

Humility

Terrific. *Humility.* Just what I needed to hear, right? *Good grief,* I thought.

I'd already been plenty humiliated, thank you very much. I'd had enough humiliation to last a lifetime.

When I got back to my apartment, I saw my cell phone sitting on my kitchen counter. Which told me just how shook up I'd been over my revelation about Lacy and our breakup. I *never* went anywhere without my phone.

I checked my voicemail and found I'd missed a call while I was out walking. I played back the voicemail.

It was from the police.

You know the expression "my heart leapt"? My first memory of experiencing that feeling was at age eighteen, when I tore into the end zone and knew I'd completed the winning touchdown for that state championship. *Yesss!*

That's exactly how it felt now.

I punched in the digits and waited through two rings, then nearly shouted my name when someone picked up.

"Hey, Mr. Barab." I recognized the voice. It was the same desk sergeant I'd spoken to when I reported the theft. "We found your car."

A flood of relief poured through me.

Naturally I was thrilled to have my racecar back, to say nothing of that precious file box, assuming the thief had left it untouched. More than that, though, it was a *sign*. A good sign. A great sign.

Things were finally starting to turn around!

"Where is it?" I practically babbled. "When can I pick it up?"

"About that," the desk sergeant said.

My heart decelerated from sixty to zero.

"The vehicle is at Ernie's Towing right now," he said, "in the back lot. It's in pretty bad shape."

There was a moment of silence.

Then he said, "You should be able to get at least a couple hundred dollars for parts. You just have to go in and sign for it."

I cleared my throat and asked about the file box on the floor of the front passenger seat.

"Ah, no, Mr. Barab, no possessions in the vehicle. In fact, the seats themselves are gone."

The *seats*?

"It's in pretty bad shape," he repeated.

8. DAD

That Sunday I climbed into the used Civic—which I'd now purchased from the rental place with my "few hundred for parts," plus some of my dwindling cash—and went for my once-a-month visit to the nursing home to see Dad.

After Mom died, Dad started going rapidly downhill. The diagnosis: early-onset Alzheimer's. Within a month he was in a home. I would go see him on the last Sunday of every month, rain or shine. I'd been doing this now for close to five years.

On these visits he would generally slip in and out of lucidity. Lately it had been more out than in. Any coherent conversation we might manage would soon fall off to little more than a trickle, which was downright eerie, given the torrent of words that used to pour out of him.

I remembered Dad—with some fondness, to be honest—as someone who always had an opinion, and who held "a very high opinion of his opinion," as Mom would joke. Dad was happy to hold forth on anything and everything. And he was no dummy, either; he read like a demon and knew a ton. His opinions were usually spot-on, or at least well-informed.

No more. Now, if Dad had any firm opinions rattling around in that old noggin, he kept them to himself. Most of the time, he didn't even know who I was, and I would just sit and silently watch Dad's movie with him.

Today I'd already tried some conversation and was met with nothing but blank stares and a hostile "Who are you?" So now, there I was, sitting and watching.

It was always a prison break movie. *Cool Hand Luke. The Great Escape. Papillon. Escape from Alcatraz. The Defiant Ones.*

I once asked Dad in one of his few lucid moments why he always watched prison break films. "A man can dream, can't he?" he replied with a sly grin. Dad had never held a high opinion of nursing homes.

He had a rotation of these films, watched them every day, over and over. Lucid or not, he'd seen them so often that he knew all the lines by heart. Sometimes he would murmur them along with the actors. To be honest, I found this unnerving.

Today it was *The Shawshank Redemption*.

"Rehabilitated?" Morgan Freeman was saying. *"Well, now, let me see. You know, I don't have any idea what that means."*

"Well," the parole board interviewer began, *"it means you're ready—"*

And suddenly Dad chimed in, delivering the words in a clear, firm voice and in perfect sync with Morgan Freeman:

"I know what you think it means, Sonny . . ."

And he proceeded to go through the whole scene, matching the actor beat for beat, inflection for inflection.

". . . I want to try to talk some sense to him, tell him the way things are. But I can't. That kid's long gone, and this old man is all that's left. I got to live with that—"

All at once the TV went blank.

I glanced over at Dad. He was holding the remote and staring straight at me.

My skin went all gooseflesh. He'd never done anything like this before.

"What would you say?" he growled, looking me directly in the eye.

"Dad?" I wasn't sure whether to be thrilled or freaked out. "You know who I am?"

"What would you say?" Dad repeated, insistent.

"What would I say? Say about what?"

"To your twenty-year-old self. To that young, stupid kid. If you could talk some sense to him. Tell him the way things are. What would you tell him?"

I just stared at him. Dad hadn't spoken in complete sentences for close to three years.

"*I* know," he continued, and he gave a grim, knowing nod. "I know damn well what I'd say. *Son*, I would say, *don't be so sure.*"

"So sure? Of what?"

When he didn't reply, I tried again.

"Don't be so sure of what, Dad?"

"*Less certainty,*" he said, his voice already faltering. "*More compassion. Less certainty.*"

He eased back against his pillow and nodded off to sleep, leaving the rest of the conversation for his son to carry on alone.

I sat there in that crummy nursing home room for a full ten minutes, staring at my drooling, snoring dad. Then stood and quietly slipped out of the room.

Climbed into my used Civic and started the forty-five-minute drive back to my apartment.

More compassion. Less certainty.

I thought about those four words, and where I'd heard them before, or something like them.

About half an hour into my drive, I remembered.

9. IMPEDIMENTS OF THE APOCALYPSE

I hadn't thought about the Coach for quite a while. Years, maybe.

The Coach was a man of many talents. He taught math during the morning hours and drilled our football team in the afternoons and on weekends. When the drama department needed some special effects for a production, it was always the Coach who worked out the mechanics. He played banjo and told jokes in the annual faculty talent show, and he was so good everyone would urge him to consider going pro.

The Coach also put in time three or four days a week working with a group we used to refer to as the "slow kids," meaning those students who had trouble reading or struggled with other learning issues. I felt bad for the "slow kids"; reading and language skills always came super easy to me, and I just couldn't comprehend how it could not be the same way for everyone.

As I may have mentioned, I played quarterback for our high school team. Not to brag, but I was pretty good. "Bob is an outstanding athlete," I remember the Coach telling my dad one Saturday when he picked me up from practice. "Which is great for us. I'm not so sure it's good for him."

I remember being confused by that remark. I asked the Coach about it at practice the next Monday.

He took me aside.

"You look at your fullback," he said, "your receivers, your second-string quarterback. Those kids work like the dickens to get what comes natural to you. You got talent, Bob. Real talent. And it's precisely 'cause of that that you've never had to work at it as hard as the others. I worry you'll take that talent for granted."

Honestly, I thought that was pretty rich, coming from a talent like him. And besides, I didn't agree. I didn't think I took anything for granted. It was just that I'd always been a very goal-driven kid, and I worked hard at the stuff I wanted to accomplish.

The Coach was long gone now; he died from a stroke a few years after I graduated. I didn't even hear about it until after the funeral had come and gone.

What brought the Coach to mind now, as I made that lonely drive back to the city, was another remark he'd made to my dad that same Saturday afternoon.

"I'd like to see Bob being a little less sure of himself," he said. I remembered how Dad and I had both rolled our eyes back then.

Now Dad was sounding an awful lot like the Coach.

More compassion, less certainty...

Ten minutes from home I slammed my foot on the brakes.

Cars honking all around me, I pulled off onto the shoulder and put my Civic in park, my heartbeat bass-drumming in my ears.

Less certainty.

Mr. Volume.

How did it go again?

Volume... age... Sufism... certainty.

The homeless guy.

I sat there, heedless of the traffic whizzing by, and

tried to make sense out of something that made no sense at all.

Volume . . . age—

Only what if I'd heard that one wrong? What if it wasn't "age" he said? What if it was—

"Rage," I said aloud to the windshield.

That was the word Lacy had used.

You don't talk, she'd said. *You rage.*

I wheeled the car around and made a beeline over to my old work neighborhood. Pulled in by the side entrance of the Mercy building, near the spot where I'd had that strange encounter with the vagrant. How long had it been since that day? I sat in my Civic and did the math. Five weeks of fruitless job searches. Another week to land that miserable gig at Jonathan's, where I'd spent almost another three weeks.

So, well over two months.

I got out and started walking. I looked everywhere, all around the outside of the hospital complex.

He wasn't there.

Which shouldn't have surprised me. I didn't remember ever having seen him before that day, or since, so chances were good he didn't frequent the hospital grounds with any regularity. But maybe he was somewhere else in the same general neighborhood.

I went door to door.

Not every place was open on a Sunday, but enough to make up a search that took a solid three hours.

I went into the Bitter Brew and talked with the waitstaff there. The framing shop. The stationers. The used bookstore. The upscale French restaurant and the inexpensive Thai place. Up and down that block, and the next, and the one beyond that.

He was nowhere.

I did find a few people who knew exactly who I was talking about, who remembered seeing him out on the street at some point—but not recently. As best I could tell, no one had seen him since the day he and I ran into each other. He seemed to have vanished.

I hoofed it back to my car and slowly drove home. Made myself a simple dinner, then sat in my over-stuffed chair, staring up at my faux mantlepiece, where that twenty-dollar bill still sat staring back at me.

Volume . . . rage . . . Sufism . . . certainty.

I couldn't begin to guess where "Sufism" was supposed to fit into the sequence. What did Sufism have to do with anything? Were there any actual Sufis even living in America? I didn't know.

"Why am I even thinking about this?" I said aloud. "It's all just a bunch of gibberish, anyway!"

Besides, I had more pressing concerns, right? Like, for instance, what to do about the unfolding apocalypse of my life.

I pried myself out of my chair, went over to the mantel, and moved a picture over to cover the twenty-dollar bill so I wouldn't have to look at it.

10. BORN TO LEAD

My severance pay from Mercy had run out. I had to leave my exquisite bachelor pad. Moved into an efficiency in a cheaper neighborhood.

Over the next few weeks I managed to land a management position of sorts, overseeing inventory at a warehouse on the outskirts of town. But it was a crap job and the pay was less than subsistence.

The last thing I wanted to do was go see Uncle Bill, but I didn't really see that I had a choice.

Uncle Bill was my one living relative. Sis was gone, three years now. ODed. As was Mom (cancer, five years past). Dad was "here" only in the broadest sense of the term. For all practical purposes—and right now I was facing that most practical of purposes, survival—I was alone in the world. Except for Uncle Bill.

Mom was an only child, but Dad had one brother, a dairy farmer who lived a few hours north, up in the country. Uncle Bill had done quite well for himself over the years. Kept a tight rein on the farm's finances, and through a local banker friend managed to make some modest investments that performed nicely over the years.

I drove up one late-fall weekend to see him under the pretense of wanting to "catch up," family to family. But we both knew why I was really there.

He listened to my tale of woe, nodding at every turn, his face too blank through his little wire-frame glasses for me to have a clue which way the wind was blowing. When I finished, he clapped one gnarled hand on my shoulder.

"Bob," he said, "I want you to know, I get your plight. And it makes my heart ache." He thumped one fist against his chest by way of illustration. "Blood is blood, Bob. When you live on a farm, that ain't some platitude, it's daily life. Blood is blood. I'm feeling your pain, and it hurts me, too."

Those words should have inspired hope, but coming from Uncle Bill's blank face, they had the opposite effect.

"You know, Bob," he continued, "you're a very special young man. Always have been. *Born to lead*, that's what we always said about you." He was nodding as he spoke, as if agreeing with himself. "*Born to lead*," he repeated. "You can do whatever you set your mind to, Bob Barab, and don't let anyone tell you you can't. You just have to plan your work—"

"And work my plan," I said in unison with him. That one was burned into my brain; Dad and Uncle Bill must have both gotten it from the same source.

Plan your work and work your plan.

You can do whatever you set your mind to.

The Barab family catechism.

Uncle Bill nodded again for a moment, whether to me or to himself I couldn't tell. Then he looked up at me. "You still read your Bible, son?"

I gave a shrug that could have been interpreted to mean anything.

"Ever'thing you need, son, you'll find in those pages. 'God helps those who help themselves.' You remember that one, right? Might be the most powerful handfulla words in the whole dang book."

He regarded me through his granny glasses for a moment. He nodded again, then took a big breath and let it out again, in a sort of glad-that's-all-settled way.

"I'm not gonna give you any dough, Bob. I wanna do

it, Lord knows I wanna do it. But I'm not. This is your opportunity, son. I'm not gonna take it away from you."

And before you could say "Hail Mary pass," my hopes of a goodwill, all-in-the-family loan were gone.

Maybe you've heard this one.

Guy walks into a bookstore, asks the clerk where he can find the self-help section.

Clerk goes, "If I told you, it would defeat the purpose."

Ha-ha.

I got into my battered Civic and drove back to the city in what I could only describe as, okay, a *rage*, but also with something else sitting in the pit of my stomach, some feeling that I couldn't quite name.

It took me nearly the entire car ride to put my finger on what it was, and even when I did, I had a hard time accepting it.

I was frightened.

First I was lonely—and now I was frightened? *Who is this guy?* I thought. I couldn't relate to these feelings. They weren't emotions I even recognized, let alone identified with. But there they were.

It was a lonely, frightened Bob behind the wheel of this crappy used car.

Most of all, I was *confused*.

I'd done a good job leading my team at Mercy. No, not a good job, a great job. Right? And that was an enormous challenge we'd taken on. There were few people in the city who could pull that off, maybe as few as you could count on one hand. Not a boast, just the truth. I was good at what I did, seriously good.

I'd led that team to triumph.

Just like I'd led my football team to that state championship.

I was, as Uncle Bill had pointed out, *born to lead*.

So what happened?

In math class, the Coach used to talk about what he called the "1 in 60 rule." It had to do with calculating the navigational error in an airplane's flight path, and it went something like this:

> *With each degree of arc in error, you will end up roughly one mile off course for every sixty you travel.*

"And that's not just about flying a plane," the Coach would tell us. "It applies to navigating your life path, too.

"Let's say you make one insignificant error in

judgment. Call it one degree of arc. No big deal. You can hardly even see that, right? But then let's say you continue uncorrected on that path, making that same one-degree error in judgment, on and on for sixty miles down the road. Suddenly you find you're a mile away from where you thought you were headed.

"Now, let's say you're not going sixty miles. Let's say you're going from JFK to LAX, which is about 2,800 miles. Let's say you're flying there for an important meeting. Call it a meeting with your destiny. You take off right on time—but you're one degree off. By the time you reach LA, that one degree of uncorrected error has taken you more than forty-five miles off course.

"That one 'insignificant error' in judgment, perpetuated over the length of your journey, could make the difference between arriving at your meeting with destiny—or using your airline seat as a flotation device."

Okay.

I got the concept.

What I didn't get was, where the heck did I veer so badly off course?

By the time I was back in my little one-room apartment I'd decided, with great reluctance, that it was time to raid my investment account.

A few years back, I'd made a shrewd investment with an old high school buddy. Jim was a big hulk of a guy, an awesome left tackle, always had my flank. I trusted him.

It was a new cryptocurrency. "Like Bitcoin," Jimmy had told me, "but hardly anyone knows about it yet, so it's a lot cheaper to get in—and it has a way bigger upside."

I got Jim on his home phone and, after the requisite small talk, I told him I'd had a string of reversals in my career and was in a bit of a bind, cash-wise. "Hate to do it, Jimmy, but I think I'm gonna have to tap that investment account."

There was a brief silence on the line.

"Jimmy?"

"Yeah, still here. I was gonna call you about that."

My stomach dropped.

"Why? What happened?" I said, trying not to sound as panicked as I felt. I'd poured every dollar of savings into that investment account.

"It's good news and bad news. And don't worry— the good news is *really* good. And the bad news is no big deal."

The knot in my stomach loosened, but only slightly.

"The good news is," he continued, "the thing behaved exactly the way we thought it would. Better, actually. A *lot* better. Your account value is way up, higher even than I'd hoped."

The knot in my stomach loosened some more. "And the bad news?"

"We had a fire in the building. Our records are all toast. Literally."

"Okay," I said. "Exactly what does that mean? You've got everything on backup somewhere in the cloud, right? Tell me you've got off-site backup, Jim—"

"Of course we do. Everything but the individual passwords. Security protocol, remember? We each kept our own personal passwords separate from everything else and stored them ourselves. That's how you do it with crypto."

I remembered. If anyone ever managed to steal or copy your personal password, they could go in and clean out your account, so you had to keep it safe and in your own possession.

"Like I said, the bad news is minor. All our accounts are safe as Fort Knox. Just come in with your password, whenever you want, and we can cash in and pull out whatever you need. And the numbers are big, Bob. Crazy big. You're gonna be a happy man."

I let out a huge breath of relief.

"You're an animal, Jimmy! An ever-lovin' animal!

I'll be in with that thumb drive first thing Monday morning."

I clicked off and sat back in my favorite chair, one of the few remaining furnishings I'd been able to fit into my crosstown efficiency.

Back when Jimmy first created the account, he'd given me my own copy of that personal password on a dedicated thumb drive. Neither of us ever thought we'd need it. But hey, that was why you had backups to your backups, right?

Now where had I stashed that thumb drive?

I got up and went through my desk. Bookshelves. Closets. Turned the place upside down. Finally I remembered where I kept it.

In my office.

Which meant it was in that file box.

The one I stashed on the floor of the front passenger seat.

Of my racecar.

The knot in my stomach twisted into a rock-hard lump.

My money was safe, all sitting right there in my account. Way more than I'd even hoped for.

And I'd never be able to access it.

11. THE TRUTH

I guess I went a little crazy.

I gave notice at the warehouse, sold off a bunch of my cherished kitchen appliances for cash to live on, and began to pour every waking moment into trying to work out exactly what it was Cynthia Sharpe had done to me.

I know, I know. This was not a healthy move. I knew that. In my defense, I was at my wits' end. I suppose my logic was, if I could reverse engineer just what had happened, maybe I could find a way to undo the damage.

And start putting my life back together again.

My attempts to talk to people in my old department

led nowhere; nobody would speak to me. A few threatened to turn me in for harassment. I tried to hack into Cynthia's email, but I'd never really been a nuts-and-bolts guy, and I couldn't penetrate my own system. Gavin could've done it. I wished I could call on him again. But at this point I was in this alone. I still had enough sense to see that.

I began to follow her.

It's not like it sounds—I mean, I wasn't *stalking* her. I just hung around in the neighborhood of Mercy, kept my eyes open when she came and went. Just to see if she talked to anyone or did anything . . . I don't know. Suspicious.

This went on for maybe three weeks.

Then one day I decided to do a little close-up reconnaissance.

Shortly before her habitual lunchtime, I slipped into the Bitter Brew and set myself up at a back table with a coffee and a magazine. And waited.

Ten minutes went by. Fifteen. Then twenty. Finally, thirty-eight minutes and two coffee refills after I first sat down, in came Cynthia, gliding up to the counter as silent as a cat.

She put in her lunch order, then took her coffee over to her usual table, up by the front window. And so help me, not two minutes had gone by before she turned around and looked right in my direction. There wasn't even time to react. She'd caught me glaring straight at her.

She got up, walked over to my table, and sat down across from me. Looked me up and down with an expression that was somewhere between pity and horror. I hadn't been sleeping well; I suppose I looked pretty terrible.

"Bob, what . . . happened to you?"

I laid it all out there. "I know what you did, *Sin*-thia. I don't know exactly how, but I'll figure it out. You always wanted me gone. I was always too much of a threat to you. And you found a way!"

She stared at me like I'd lost my mind.

"Bob, I don't have the faintest idea what you're talking about."

"Go ahead, deny it. I know it was you who convinced Norman I was angling for his job—and don't think I won't make sure Norman knows it, too, and when I do, you'll be sorry. *Both* of you will be sorry!"

She took a long look at me. Shook her head. Then said, her voice calm and quiet, "You want to know why you were fired?"

"I *know* why I was fired," I hissed. "More or less."

"More or less," she repeated. "Uh-huh. Let me ask you this. Why did you call it the Hero Project?"

"What do you mean, why did—*I* didn't . . . we *all* called it that."

"No, Bob, we didn't all call it that. You did. You picked out that name and rammed it through committee. So tell me, what made you choose that name in particular? 'Hero'?"

"You know very well why we called it that."

"Humor me."

I explained, even though she knew the answer as well as I did. "Because it would let doctors do what they were there to do, instead of battling with a briar patch of legacy data systems. It would let them be the heroes they were groomed to be."

She kept looking at me but didn't say a word.

"And it was configured like a sandwich," I added.

Somehow it sounded foolish now, when I said it out loud.

Finally, Cynthia sighed. "Hopeless," she said, and she got up from her chair to leave.

"What," I said.

"You go ahead and tell yourself that."

"What are you saying?"

She sat back down and looked at me again. "Bob, you called it the Hero Project to make *yourself* the hero. It was always about you. The way you told it, the whole thing was your idea, your brainstorm, your execution."

I didn't say anything, but the expression on my face must have conveyed what I was thinking. *Well? Wasn't that the truth? Wasn't it pretty much my brainchild?*

"You see?" she said, pointing one perfect Cynthia finger at the expression on my face. "You still think that, even now! Do you even know how many hundreds of hours Gavin put in? How much of the underlying structure of the whole thing came out of his brain? Or who worked out the actual solutions to all those incompatibilities? Easily a dozen people poured their ingenuity and creative ideas, their sweat and blood, into that project."

"And I totally gave them credit—"

"You totally did not! You made a few vague gestures to 'the team.' Never citing any specific names. Never acknowledging the individuals involved. It was always about you. And it pissed people off. *You* pissed people off. The only surprise, the day you were fired? Was that it didn't happen months earlier."

I struggled to process this all. It just didn't add up.

"I don't . . . help me out here, Cynthia. I mean, *why?* Why did they fire me?"

"You really don't know, do you. The money, Bob."

The money? I stared at her. What money?

And she told me what happened.

There was a misappropriation of funds. Not an enormous amount, less than $50,000. But way too much to be a bookkeeping error.

It happened during the conversion from the old systems to the new integrated system. Purchase orders, invoices, interdepartmental communications . . . somewhere in there a small black hole opened up, and over the course of ten months, nearly fifty grand slipped through that hole, never to be seen again.

"The hospital absorbed the financial hit," she said. "But they couldn't afford the hit in credibility. They had to keep it quiet. Especially because they couldn't prove who the culprit was. Not definitively. Still, the circumstantial evidence . . ."

"What are you saying? That the circumstantial evidence pointed to *me*?"

She shrugged. "Nice car, upscale apartment. Classy threads."

"Hey," I said. "I like nice things—I've never hid that, or apologized for it, either. But I earned every penny. I worked *hard* for that apartment!"

"And," she went on as if I hadn't spoken, "all the invoices and purchase orders flowed through your office at some point."

"Yeah, but . . ." I stopped. That was true. But so what? This still made no sense to me.

"The thing is, Bob"—she leaned forward as she said this next part—"the thing is, it was you who claimed ownership of the whole project. *You* were the one who made it about you. You made yourself into the single most obvious suspect."

"That's crazy! They had no proof!"

"No, they didn't, and they didn't really need any. Because who else could have done it? Who else *would* have done it?"

I stared down at the dregs of my coffee.

Who indeed.

Who, on our entire team, would do such a thing? And leave me twisting in the wind, taking the blame? Who would be that cold? That devious?

I straightened up and stared her in the eye.

"I can't believe it," I hissed. "I can't believe you would stoop so low."

She stood and took one more pitying look at me.

"Open your eyes, Bob," she said.

And without another word, she turned and walked out of the café.

After Cynthia left, I sat at my empty table for what was probably no more than fifteen minutes but felt like an hour.

I thought about storming back to Mercy and demanding to see Norman so I could explain myself, explain that I had nothing to do with the fifty grand, that I hadn't even known about it until now. Park myself at reception, if I had to. Force them to let me in. And if he wouldn't listen, then hire a phalanx of litigators to fight it.

But I knew I wouldn't do any of that. After all this time, who would listen? And besides, I'd never be able to prove I didn't do this thing, because it's impossible to prove a negative.

I remembered that last phone call I'd had with Norman the morning after I'd been fired, when I tried to get in to see him. "Don't make me get the board of directors involved," he'd said. "Or worse." I remembered thinking, *What was worse than involving the hospital's entire board of directors?*

Now I knew.

Who handled embezzlement? The city police? State prosecutor's office? The FBI? I didn't want to find out.

Finally I got up and walked into the men's room out back, where I leaned on the sink and splashed cold water on my face. I stared at myself in the mirror and thought about Cynthia's parting words.

Open your eyes, Bob.

Open my eyes to what?

I'd always thought of Cynthia as a master manipulator. But was that really true? Had she ever given any solid evidence of being that devious?

Not really, now that I thought about it.

In fact, not at all. Cynthia was brusque, acerbic, often abrasive. She didn't give two hoots what other people thought about her. But she didn't make any effort to hide it, either. Cynthia'd had a nickname, when I first arrived at Mercy: Ms. Wizzy-wig, after the old computer term: WYSIWYG.

What you see is what you get.

Was she, in fact, duplicitous? Conniving? Not really.

Not at all.

So where did I get that idea about her?

And then it came to me, in a single screaming, horrifying epiphany.

That comment about Cynthia, the one about how she could cut you on Friday and you wouldn't know you were bleeding till Monday? Now I remembered where I'd heard that. I recalled those words being whispered into my ear in the midst of some long and boring departmental meeting.

Being whispered into my *right* ear, by the person sitting directly next to me.

My right-hand man.

My man Friday.

It wasn't Cynthia at all. It had never been Cynthia. It was David.

I fell back against the men's room wall and sank to a sitting position on the floor.

My dad used to do magic tricks for Sis and me when we were little. Later, when I was a teen, he explained how it all worked. "It's not about the tricks themselves, Bob. It's all about getting the other person's mind off what you're doing. You call their attention to that thing over there, so they don't notice what your hand is doing over here."

It was all a trick, a con. And I was the mark.

All the invoices and purchase orders flowed through your office at some point.

David had distracted me with flattery and praise.

How could I have been so stupid?

Easy: I *made* myself stupid.

My own ego, my own pride, had made me blind to the truth of what was right in front of my face.

The homeless guy was right.

Tripped ... o'er yourself.

12. BEING SPECIAL

You're special, Bob.

It was something my parents had told me for as long as I could remember, and I'd always believed it.

Sitting there sprawled on the men's room floor of the Bitter Brew, I remembered the words, as vivid as if I were hearing them spoken out loud, right that moment.

You're special, Bob. Don't let anyone tell you different. You've got something nobody else has.

I know, every kid's dad tells them that. But he wasn't just saying it. It was true. I did have something other kids didn't have.

My name.

Bob.

Barab.

Both *palindromes*. Spelled the same backwards and forwards.

B-O-B.

B-A-R-A-B.

Palindromes.

I know that probably doesn't seem like a big deal to you, but you have to understand: in our family, it was always a very big deal indeed.

I was "Bob" even when I was a toddler. Never "Bobby" or, God forbid, "Robert." It's right there on my birth certificate. You can look it up in the city records. "Bob."

The same backwards and forwards.

My sister's name, "Sis," wasn't a nickname. That was her actual name. Right there on her birth certificate. Just like mine.

Our parents were named Albert and Susannah— but I'd never heard them called that, not once, not by their friends, not even by their colleagues. They'd always been "Mom" and "Dad." (Or "Pop," when he was feeling playful.)

That was why I always drove a Civic.

C-I-V-I-C.

Until I decided it was time to upgrade and got

myself a nice Toyota, which I always referred to as my "racecar."

R-A-C-E-C-A-R.

Or simply, "a Toyota."

A-T-O-Y-O-T-A.

Once, in my early twenties, I almost bought a kayak, purely because it was called a "kayak," until I realized just before slapping down my credit card that I didn't especially love being out on the water.

Our everyday language at home was peppered with code words like "level," "tenet," "radar," and "deified," and short phrases like "top spot," "my gym," and "never odd or even." Sis and I got to the point where we didn't even notice we were doing it—"Don't nod." "I did, did I?"

Dad and I used to have entire conversations that consisted of nothing but palindromes.

"Yo, banana boy!"

"Go hang a salami, I'm a lasagna hog."

Or:

"Do geese see God?"

"Sit on a potato pan, Otis."

Or:

"Was it a car or a cat I saw?"

"Ed, *I* saw Harpo Marx ram Oprah W aside!"

They made no sense, but that wasn't the point. They were palindromes.

Our special family code.

When I first got to Mercy, there was a guy who insisted on calling me "Bobby." Drove me nuts. Thankfully, that guy left after six months.

Of course, there were plenty of other Bobs walking around in the world. And Nans, and Eves, and Hannahs. An Otto here and there. I even knew an Idi once. But none of them had what I did. A *double* palindrome.

B-o-b B-a-r-a-b.

Which was indisputable evidence of my specialness, right?

And now, sitting there on the floor of that public restroom in the Bitter Brew, it all felt so . . . foolish.

I struggled to my feet and stood at the sink again, staring into the mirror.

Really, Bob? Because your name can flip-flop like a weather vane, that makes you *special*?

Another memory of the Coach came flooding back. Sometimes—in math class, at football practice, even now and then in the cafeteria at lunch—he'd launch into one of his philosophical homilies.

"Watch out for isms," he would say. "Racism, sexism, ageism. Classism. Nationalism. Some are obviously pernicious, but they all have the potential to steer you into bad territory, because they're all ways of grabbing onto the idea that you're different from other people, and therefore better than other people. That you're special. I-S-M—'I'm a Special Me.'

"And that's the most dangerous ism of all. The one that's easiest to fall into, and therefore the one you have to be the most vigilant about. *Selfism*."

"Selfism," I whispered into the men's room mirror.

And a cold chill went up my spine.

The homeless guy.

He wasn't saying "Sufism."

13. NOWHERE

What do you want from me?" I screamed into the men's room mirror. Although my throat was so dry and scratchy, it came out as more of a hoarse croak than a scream.

I'd never in my life heard anyone else use the word "selfism," other than the Coach, and he'd been gone for years now. So how did the homeless guy know the Coach's term?

How did he know Gavin would say I was "Mr. Volume"?

Or that Lacy would tell me, "You don't talk, you *rage*"?

Or that, out of the blue, my dementia-riddled father would talk to me about *certainty*?

It was like the man was time traveling—like he'd been eavesdropping on my future conversations before they happened. Déjà vu, but in reverse. And from someone who didn't even know me!

I turned on the cold water again, my hands shaking so badly I could barely work the tap. I splashed more water on my face.

This was crazy, I knew that—I mean, not crazy like stalking Cynthia was crazy, or trying to hack into her email was crazy. This was some first-class, grade A *bonkers* we were talking here. But how else could you possibly explain what that vagrant had said to me?

And on that day, of all days? The day my life started disintegrating like a cheap rug?

Oh well, I remembered thinking at the time, *at least he isn't dangerous.*

Not dangerous? Ha! Ha-ha! Somehow, the man had completely unraveled the fabric of my life!

Who *was* that guy?

Whatever happened to him?

I turned off the water spigot.

Suddenly it seemed urgent that I find the homeless man. As if my very life and future depended on it. I had to talk to him, to find out if this was all in my head or if he actually had some kind of bizarre, unexplainable insight into my life. I needed to know who he was and how he knew these things about me, and if this was all really true or just a figment of my fevered imagination.

There had to be someone who would have paid some attention to him and might have some idea where I could find him.

I dried my face off with a paper towel and looked back in the mirror again—and the moment I did the answer hit me.

Lacy!

Of course! Why had I not thought of that before? She walked in and out of that ER entrance every single day. And if there was anyone on planet earth who'd pay attention to a homeless person and see if she could help their situation in some way, it would be kindhearted Lacy.

I dashed out of the Bitter Brew and fast-walked over to the ER entrance at Mercy. It took me a few minutes to convince the intake nurse to page Lacy for me—I may have made up some insane story about her brother having been in an accident (she doesn't have a brother)—but finally she came out through the big double doors, her face painted with concern.

"Bob," she said, "what on earth—"

"I'm sorry, Lacy," I stammered, "I'm really, really sorry, I know this is nuts, but I need to ask you about someone."

I quickly explained about the guy I'd seen out by the side entrance the day I was fired, and how I'd tried to give him some money but he'd refused.

"John, you mean," she said. "That poor man."

"You know him!"

"Knew him. Only briefly. You're talking about the John Doe they found out back last April, right? They brought him inside that afternoon."

"Yes! Who is he? Where can I find him? I have to talk to him!"

She looked at me with sad eyes and shook her head. "I never knew his real name. He died that night."

I don't remember exactly what happened after that.

I know I got sick. That dry, scratchy throat I'd felt at the Bitter Brew wouldn't quit, and over the next few weeks it blossomed into something more full-blown. It was probably nothing more than your garden-variety cold or flu, but I couldn't seem to shake it.

I remember at some point moving into a still

cheaper place, a room in some boardinghouse in the rough section of town.

I don't remember anything about the place.

A year went by.

I have vague recollections of working at a few different places, all in the same general neighborhood. It seemed I'd lost the capacity to hold down any kind of job at all. Or maybe I just didn't care enough.

I couldn't remember what stage was supposed to come after "bargaining," but whatever it was, I was probably in it.

At some point I must have been kicked out of my boardinghouse, because I remember walking down some street, trying to recall where it was I was supposed to sleep that night, and then thinking, "Oh, right. Nowhere."

I would have slept in my car, but the old C-I-V-I-C was long gone by now, along with my cell phone and pretty much everything I'd owned. I have no idea what happened to my favorite overstuffed chair, but it must have moved on, too.

Vanity of vanities.

Was there anywhere I could have turned? Sure. There were any number of former colleagues and friends who probably would've let me crash at their place, at least for a while. Lacy would've put me up on her couch, if I'd asked. Or Gavin—I didn't know where he lived, but he must have lived somewhere, right? Or Jimmy, my broker friend. So why didn't I ask? Maybe I was too proud. Or maybe, after everything I'd been through, I was just afraid they would say no.

I didn't think I could take any more humiliation.

In any case, I didn't ask anyone, so when I got evicted, I stayed evicted.

I have a hazy memory of Uncle Bill offering me lodgings at his farm in exchange for work. It never even occurred to me to accept the offer.

Believe it or not, I actually had a job at this point, working the swing shift at a twenty-four-hour store, which paid me enough so that I could eat without begging.

During the days, I made it my business to research a selection of the city's finest locations for daytime repose. The bus station. The train station. Under bridges. Tucked into various alleys and enclosed walkways.

Pretty much what you'd expect.

Here's something I learned: You know that thing you've probably read about, how street people line their shoes with newspaper for insulation? That actually works pretty well. As long as you keep your feet dry. Soggy newspapers, and *boom*, before you know it, you've got infected toes.

I remembered what Lacy said that time we had breakfast. "Having a sense of humor isn't about clever punch lines—it's about having a sense of perspective. Like, seeing the irony of a situation."

How was this for irony: now *I* was the homeless guy.

Late one night, while making my nightly commute from work to nowhere, I was walking by a dark, narrow side street when I heard the unmistakable sounds of a physical struggle.

I poked my head around the corner and saw two men in the process of hassling some well-dressed gentleman. It looked like they were shaking him down. They had him against the wall, his arm twisted behind him, his face mashed up against the bricks.

I don't know why, but something about the scene triggered a blast of white-hot fury in me. My temper blew like a volcano.

"Hey, you idiots!" I yelled. "Leave the man alone!"

And they did.

Oh boy, did they ever.

They let go of the guy in the tailored suit, who

staggered off in the other direction, and came after me instead.

They grabbed me and dragged me into the alley, where they proceeded to beat me viciously until I was on my knees.

At which point they moved from fists to feet.

Eventually they left me there on the asphalt, bleeding and unconscious, a nobody in the heart of nowhere.

14. THE ER

The moment I came to, I knew where I was. Lying on my back on an ER bed.

At Mercy.

Of course.

So they took me back after all, I thought. *My master plan worked!*

I started to chuckle, but a bolt of pain shot through my ribs so sharply it left me gasping for breath. So much for a sense of humor. I closed my eyes and lay there, waiting for the agony to subside.

I must have drifted off.

Nurses and med techs came and went, checking my IV, changing my bedpan, administering meds.

"Thirsty?" a young man asked at one point. I gave a slight headshake to indicate the negative. He raised my head a little and made me drink some water anyway, through a straw. It hurt to move my mouth. A lot.

An indeterminate span of time later, I opened my eyes and Lacy was there, holding my hand.

"Oh, Bob," she said.

She gave me the weather report. My face had taken a beating. I had two broken ribs and a few bad lacerations on my back from where one of the muggers had kicked me. No internal bleeding, no serious kidney damage.

Still, judging from Lacy's face, I must have looked quite the mess.

"Should've seen . . ." I croaked.

She leaned closer. "Seen what?"

"Other guy . . ."

She sat back. "Bob, that may be the funniest thing I've ever heard you say." She grinned.

"Yay, Bob," I said weakly. I lifted my right hand a few inches and made a little flag-waving motion.

Her face grew serious. "Oh, Bob," she whispered again. "What were you thinking? They could have hurt you a lot worse. They could have *killed* you."

She told me they hadn't yet caught the two guys who beat me up, but they did talk with the man who was being assaulted when I arrived on the scene. He was the one who'd called 911. Apparently, he'd already been pretty badly hurt by the time I showed up. It was only after they'd gotten me to the hospital and IDed me that the guy realized he actually knew me.

The well-dressed gentleman those two were beating up? None other than David, my old man Friday.

David, my trusty right hand.

David, who ruined my life.

And it looked like I may have just saved his.

Could I appreciate the irony of *this* situation? Oh, yes. Yes, I could. It was almost as if life itself were whacking me over the head with a big placard that read, "*Now* do you get it?"

Although to be honest, I still wasn't sure I knew exactly what "it" was.

"He was the one, wasn't he," Lacy said. "The one who got you fired."

I gave a faint nod. "Didn't know . . ."

"You didn't know who it was? Whose skin you were saving?"

I nodded again. This was something to absorb, all right.

After a moment I said, "Don't know . . ."

"Don't know what?" She waited, and when I didn't reply she said, "You don't know if you would've stepped in to help him, if you'd known who he was?"

I gave a micron-sized shrug and winced as that searing pain shot through my ribs again.

"It doesn't matter," she said. "You still did what you did. You've got a good heart, you know that, Bob? You're an insufferable jerk, but you've got a good heart."

"Not . . . so sure."

She looked into my face for a moment, pensive. "You're not a bad person, Bob. You just get in your own way."

So I'd heard.

"I always thought . . . I was . . . *special*." It was hurting worse to talk, but I pressed on. "Nothing. Special. About me."

She leaned in and planted the carefullest, tenderest kiss on my forehead.

"You *are* special, Bob. The thing is, so is everyone."

A doctor arrived, a kindly Asian woman who looked to be younger than me. Although right then probably everyone on earth looked younger than me.

Lacy must have slipped out while the doc was checking my vitals. I didn't see her go.

"Looks like you ran into some trouble," the doc said. "That was very brave."

"Very stupid," I said through my teeth.

She laughed. "Yeah, that too. What exactly were you thinking, Mr. Barab?"

I started to heave a sigh, but the pain made that impossible. I took a few shallow breaths. "Guess I thought I was invincible."

She nodded as she made notations on her digital pad. The pad my team designed. "Turns out, you're not." She finished up her notes and looked up at me. "You gonna be okay? You have somewhere to go? Someone who can look after you for a few days?"

"Yeah," I lied.

Along with a few prescriptions, she handed me a generous bunch of high-strength Tylenol samples. Then she pressed a card into my hand. I glanced down at it.

It was for a homeless shelter.

I tried to hand it back. "Don't need this," I said.

She wouldn't take it. "Humor me," she said.

They kept me overnight for observation. I guess they were satisfied with whatever they observed, because they released me the following morning.

For the next seventy-two hours I roamed the city, aching all over from my beating. I'm not sure what I thought I was looking for, but evidently I didn't find it, because I kept on moving.

Bridges, park benches, bus stations.

I never slept for more than an hour at a time. I

found some things to eat in trash bins out behind restaurants—the French place, the Thai place, even the Bitter Brew.

And I kept moving.

At some point, I found myself standing in front of a door I'd never seen before, but I recognized it all the same. The name on the door was the same as the name on the card the young Asian doctor had pressed into my hand.

I was so tired.

So very, very tired.

I pushed open the door and stepped inside.

15. SHIPWRECKED

I spent that night at the shelter, and the next night, and the night after that. They gave me a brand-new toothbrush, so I was able to brush my teeth every night before I went to sleep. I couldn't remember the last time I'd brushed my teeth. It felt like the purest luxury I'd ever experienced.

They also had clothes on offer there, no doubt all donated, but clean and in decent shape. I was reluctant to take them up on that, though. I suppose I still had some pride.

The one thing that concerned me was the state of my feet. Natural disaster victims and homeless people share this in common: the thing they need most is clean, dry socks, yet socks are often the last thing people think of when they make donations. I didn't inspect my feet too closely, but I was pretty sure they were in bad shape.

I accepted the offer of a fresh pair of socks.

My third morning there, as I was preparing to leave—the shelter didn't keep residents on during the day—I was approached by another regular, a big man named Lucius who came from Haiti, or Jamaica, or somewhere else in that general part of the world. Lucius was a monster of a guy and would have been terrifying if he hadn't had such a gentle disposition.

"Mon," he said, "you smell samting awful. Whoo!"

This had completely escaped my notice, but clearly Lucius was right. My days on the street, in the alleyways and trash bins, had taken their inevitable toll.

The shelter offered access to showers among its amenities, but I had not yet availed myself of this luxury. By now my clothes were little more than filthy rags, and it was a wonder they still clung to my body. The idea of taking them all off and then putting them back on again on top of my freshly showered self had seemed abhorrent.

It was time for some new clothes.

On my neighborhood walk that day I located a Salvation Army store. I went inside and picked out a set of clothes for myself. Threadbare khaki pants, long-sleeved undershirt. Thin woolen gloves, slightly mismatched, with the fingers cut off. Then I spotted an item I instantly knew would be just the thing "to complete the ensemble," as they would have said at Jonathan's.

An old, orange canvas construction vest. Most of the DayGlo was even worn off.

How perfect was that?

I took my new wardrobe to the front desk and fished out the remainder of my cash reserves, which consisted of a single twenty-dollar bill.

Yes, *that* twenty-dollar bill.

How I'd held on to it through all that came before, I cannot say, but there it was.

The guy at the register handed the bill right back to me. He gave me a nod and said, "Why don't you hang on to this?"

A random act of kindness. Not the first I'd experienced, and not the last.

During the days I continued to roam the streets, but that feeling of urgency, of searching, was starting to dissipate, although a few deep aches from the beating I'd taken stayed with me. Mostly I sat on park benches and watched the world go by.

And waited for the evenings to roll around.

The shelter featured a library—all material donated, of course, and most of it dog-eared and well thumbed through. I began to spend my evenings reading, which seemed to offer tremendous solace, though I could not have said exactly why.

I had never read *The Old Man and the Sea*, and that became my first project.

It was an odd tale. An extremely unlucky old sailor and his epic battle with a huge marlin. On my first read I couldn't be sure who was supposed to be the hero, the old man or the fish. I reread it and felt just as puzzled, yet there was something about the story I found compelling.

I set it aside, promising myself a third read-through later on.

Next came a water-stained copy of *Life of Pi*, which I went through over the course of a week and enjoyed immensely.

This one was downright weird. A young Hindu boy survives a terrible storm at sea only to be forced to cross the ocean in a lifeboat also occupied by a man-eating tiger. Somehow they both reach the Americas alive, and when the tiger dashes off into the forest, the boy is sad to see him go.

I loved this one, though again, I didn't think I understood it very well at all.

Add another to the stack for a later reread.

I noticed a flimsy paperback copy of *The Little Prince*, which I read in an evening: a charming little tale of a downed aviator's encounter with an alien prince who pines for a delicate flower on his distant planet. Just as strange as *Pi*, and just as opaque, at least to my way of thinking. Yet I loved this one, too.

Next I picked up one of the handful of Bibles there and began leafing through it, more or less at random. I had never really read the Bible before and felt like most of it went over my head, but I kept at it; I especially enjoyed reading about Job and Jonah, who both went through some pretty terrible circumstances but apparently made out all right in the end. The prophet Jeremiah seemed like an exceptionally gloomy character, which strangely brought me some comfort.

Weeks went by.

We slipped from summer to fall.

Bit by bit, I started helping out around the shelter. Serving food. Cleaning up. Straightening things out in the mornings before we all debarked for the day's voyage out into the streets.

I also started getting to know the woman who ran the place, who in addition to being extremely resourceful and capable was incredibly patient. Not always an easy thing, given the diversity and unpredictable temperaments of the shelter's clientele. There were times I couldn't see how she managed it. Her face felt familiar to me, though I could not quite place her.

Anne, her name was.

Anne always showed up at the center looking well turned out—not flashy or pretentious, but quietly elegant. I learned that she lived across town in a fairly well-to-do neighborhood. In fact, only blocks from where I'd used to live. Which I figured must explain the familiarity; I didn't remember seeing her there, but perhaps we'd crossed paths.

Anne soon took an interest in my reading. One evening when I'd been leafing back and forth through my ratty old Bible for an hour, she came over and stood by me. "Interesting little collection there," she said. I looked down and realized I had three books piled next to me.

The Old Man and the Sea.

Life of Pi.

The Little Prince.

I looked up at her. "I'd never read any of them before."

She nodded thoughtfully. "All shipwreck books."

The thought had not occurred to me, but now that

she mentioned it, I supposed that was true. All three were about shipwrecks of one sort or another. So was the book of Jonah, for that matter.

And I guessed the book of Job was about a kind of shipwreck, too.

I glanced at my Bible, then up at her again. "Have you read the Bible much?"

"Some," she said.

"Maybe you can answer something for me. I'm looking for a famous passage."

She sat down next to me. "Let's see," she said. "How does it go?"

"It's one everybody knows. 'God helps those who help themselves.' I feel like an idiot, but I can't find it anywhere."

She smiled. "That's because it isn't there."

I must have stared at her, because she laughed.

"Are you sure?" I said.

"Pretty darn sure."

"Wow," I said. So much for Uncle Bill's studied piety. Apparently the "biblical" quote he'd called "the most powerful handfulla words in the whole dang book" was not actually *in* the whole dang book.

I looked over at Anne again. "Pretty sure, or really sure?"

"Oh, I'm positive," she said. "No such passage. In

fact, it pretty much says the opposite. I'd say God very much helps those who *don't* help themselves. You could call it grace. Or mercy." She smiled. "Or serendipity. An unexpected, unsought benefit that comes your way. 'Out of left field,' as people say."

She thought for a moment, then added, "Perhaps God *is* left field."

I told her a little about Uncle Bill and my family creed. *Plan your work and work your plan.* She nodded. "I've heard that one. Here's another, though, and I think it probably predates yours: *man plans and God laughs.*"

We laughed together, each of us at our own follies, I suppose. It felt strange to laugh. Unfamiliar, but good, too. I couldn't remember the last time I'd done it.

"Okay," I said. "Here's something else I used to hear. *You can do anything you set your mind to.*"

She frowned as she considered that. "I'm sure that's true," she said. "But what if your mind is wrong?"

"Wow," I said again. "Never thought of it that way."

What if your mind is wrong?

What if your flight plan is off by one degree of arc, as the Coach would say.

Thinking of the Coach was what did it. I suddenly realized why Anne's face was so familiar. We'd gone to school together!

Anne was one of the Coach's "slow kids."

I had no idea what it said under Anne's photo in our yearbook, but I very much doubted it said, "To a Born Leader." Yet here we were, she and I.

I was homeless.

And she was running this place.

A humbling thought.

Anne went off to attend to another regular, leaving me alone with my little library of shipwrecks. I opened the Bible again and leafed through it randomly, from back to front. On impulse, I turned to the title page, and found something I hadn't noticed before. In the white space just under the title "Holy Bible," someone had scribbled an inscription, just a few lines, with a felt-tip pen:

HUMILITY
is when you get your ego in perspective.

HUMILIATION
is when you don't, and the world has to do it for you.

And farther down, toward the bottom of the page, was another note in the same hand, which I now recognized as Merl's scrawl:

P.S. "Humility" comes from the same root word as "humus."
We all come from the dust of the earth.

16. SANTIAGO

The months drifted by like clouds in a still sky. Autumn lay down, closed its eyes, and became winter.

In the patch of lawn out behind the shelter, Anne kept a small vegetable garden. I'd started tending it a bit, in the early mornings before leaving for the day, and again in the late afternoons before dinner. With the onset of winter, the garden, too, closed its eyes and went to sleep, but I kept up my routine of going out back and spending a little time out there each day, sitting on an overturned onion bucket and watching the clouds.

One morning when I stepped outside, I noticed a

bird lying dead on the ground, a foot or so out from
the building's back wall, below a large windowpane.
The day was sunny, despite the bitter cold, and, as it
happened, cloudless. The sky was reflected brightly in
the glass.

My guess was, the bird had lost its orientation and
crashed into the window.

Leaning in to pick it up, I saw that it wasn't dead
after all, but only stunned. I knelt to take a closer look.
When I drew close, it struggled weakly.

I stood, went inside, and rummaged around out
behind the kitchen until I found a shallow berry crate,
which I lined with an old torn shirt from Anne's ragbag
and brought back outside.

When I reached under the bird to lift it into the
crate, I saw that one wing hung at an awkward angle.

Gently, I lifted the bird into the crate and brought
it inside, where I showed it to Anne, who examined
it and confirmed that the wing was broken. While I
watched, she carefully bound the little creature's wing
snug against its body with a strip cut from an Ace ban-
dage, then checked to make sure the bird's breathing
was unhindered and it could still move its legs and its
other wing.

I didn't know how she knew to do this, but by this
time nothing Anne could do would have surprised me.

She told me it could take as little as three or four weeks for the wing to mend itself. "But only if the little vagrant keeps its strength up. It'll have to eat."

I'd never heard Anne use the word "vagrant" before. She always referred to all of us regulars as "residents," and her transient drop-ins as "guests" or "visitors."

I asked her, what made her call our bird a vagrant?

"It's a term in ornithology," she said. "It means a bird that has strayed or been blown off its usual range or migratory route."

She nodded in the direction of the cold outdoors beyond the window.

"It's February," she added. "All the other birds of his kind are long gone south. This little guy got lost."

Shelter for a vagrant, I thought.

Another shipwreck.

Over the next few weeks, I watched over our littlest guest. At first, he wouldn't eat, but soon I got him to take little gulps of warmed soup stock through a medicine dropper, then eventually bits of seeds and nuts. Anne warned me that it was possible his wing would not fully heal and that he might never be able to fly again.

"Don't—" she said, and I think she was about to say, "Don't get your hopes up," but she took one look at my face and said nothing more.

I named him Santiago, but I kept the name to myself.

One day Lucius said something that startled me.

For the past few months, the other regulars had begun coming to me and looking for guidance in various matters. Steering newcomers my way, getting my take on minor disputes, things like that. Almost as if they were looking up to me.

At first, I thought I had to be imagining this. Nobody there had any reason to look to me for guidance in these matters, or in anything, really. It seemed to me I'd pretty much made a hash out of everything I'd ever touched. But it kept happening.

I sought out Lucius and asked him if it was just my projection or if this was really true.

He nodded. "Dey trust you, Bobby."

"Why would they do that?" I wondered aloud.

"Dey know you's one of us," he said.

All the rest of that day, I thought about what he said.

One of us.

That's what I was: a vagrant, blown off my path. Just like the others.

Late that afternoon, sitting outside in the garden with Santiago at my feet, another thought struck me: I didn't think I'd ever really experienced that sense of being "one of us" before. Not at Mercy, not at any of the jobs that came before Mercy. Not in business school or college, not in high school. Not on the football squad.

I'd always thought that to be a leader, you needed to fly above the rest, to stay apart from the herd. To stand out.

I thought about the last thing Lacy had said to me, before I was discharged from the hospital.

You are *special, Bob. The thing is, so is everyone.*

And then another Lacy memory surfaced: driving home to my old apartment after dropping her off at Mercy, reeling from what I'd learned over our breakfast of omelets, being stunned at the feeling of loneliness and not knowing what to do with it because I didn't think I'd ever felt it before.

Now, thinking back on it all, it seemed to me that, in fact, I'd been lonely my whole life.

Up until now, at least.

Santiago rustled his wings, made an awkward chirp, and all at once took to the air. As I watched him disappear over the horizon, I heard the soft babble of dinner preparations behind me, Anne's voice quietly reproaching someone for a coarse joke, and Lucius's unmistakable laugh.

Dey trust you, Bobby. Dey know you's one of us.

About that "Bobby" thing.

Not long after I first started coming to the shelter, someone called me Bobby, and I almost corrected him—but something stopped me. The next day others were doing it, too. I expected it to drive me nuts, but strangely, it didn't. Before long it had caught on throughout the shelter and everyone was calling me Bobby.

Except Anne. For some reason, she always called me Robert. I didn't correct her, either.

I even thought I might change it one day, legally I mean. I found I liked the sound of "Robert."

Or maybe I just liked the sound of it when she said it.

17. FEVER

I was jolted out of sleep by the sound of someone bellowing and thrashing on the floor next to me. It took me a moment to realize this was no nightmare.

It was Lucius.

He was having some kind of seizure.

In an instant I was at his side, struggling to grasp him by the shoulders. He was drumming his limbs against the floor and letting out unearthly groans, like an outboard motor trying not to stall.

I froze. What were you supposed to do for someone having an epileptic seizure? I couldn't remember.

"Get something in his mouth!" someone shouted

in my ear. He was attempting (and failing) to hold Lucius's legs down. "A belt or something!"

My brain raced, trying to remember what the Coach had taught us in our high school first aid classes.

"No!" I shouted back. "Don't restrain him! Just get him on his side!" The two of us started rolling Lucius over onto one side. We couldn't do it—the big man was just too strong. A third guy hustled over to join us, and just as I turned to make room for him, Lucius let out a roar and kicked out with one leg.

I felt a stab of pain shoot up my back.

"Get something under his head!" the first guy shouted at me. Pushing away the pain, I snatched up my orange vest, bunched it into a makeshift pillow, and levered it under Lucius's massive head. It was like lifting a rock the size of a VW.

It took five of us, but we got our friend safe and under control. Anne had already called 911; when they arrived a few minutes later, they assessed his condition and said he would probably be fine, but just to be on the safe side, they'd take him to the hospital for over-night observation.

Anne threw me a grateful look, and I nodded, too whipped to smile.

I fell back onto my cot, exhausted, figuring I'd have some major bruises to answer for the next day.

This prediction proved accurate.

At dawn the next morning, after a few hours of trying to find a position that would let me sleep, I arose from my cot with a searing headache. White-hot bolts of pain shot up and down my back, which felt broken, but I could stand. Someone from the overnight staff looked at me with concern. "You gonna be okay, Bobby?"

I nodded, pulled on my beaten-up orange construction vest, and went out into the city. I figured walking would help work out the kinks.

This prediction did *not* prove entirely accurate. What walking did, in fact, was wear me out. A few hours later, I ended up falling asleep under one of my old bridges, feeling slightly nauseated and dizzy.

It wasn't until the sun woke me late that morning that I worked out what had happened. Those wounds in my back from the alleyway assault months earlier: they must have reopened and gotten infected.

Now I had a raging fever.

I thought about making my way back to the shelter and getting help from Anne, but that was clear on the other side of town. I didn't think I could make it that far. I needed to get to a walk-in clinic or maybe an emergency room.

I looked around to get my bearings and saw that I wasn't too far from Mercy.

It was a warm April morning.

I started to walk.

It took me nearly two hours, way longer than it should have, because I had to stop and rest every five or ten minutes.

My breathing grew labored.

The nausea grew worse.

I made it as far as the back of the building, near the underground garage entrance. By this time I was stopping every fifty yards or so, and didn't think I could walk a step farther without taking a minute or two to regroup. To gather my strength.

I must have lain there for another hour.

I was dimly aware of a few passing pedestrians tossing coins at my feet. One or two tried to converse with me, I think, and asked if I needed some help. I don't remember responding.

Then there was a stretch with no people at all.

I waited.

For what, I didn't know, not yet.

Finally the silence was broken by the sound of a door being kicked open and then slammed shut. A young man emerged from the building, heading my way, muttering angrily under his breath, not looking where he was going.

Carrying a file box in his arms.

And that was when I finally understood.

Finally understood all of it.

That homeless man I'd seen so long ago, on this very spot—he hadn't been drunk, or out of his mind. He'd been on the edge of delirium.

He'd had a raging fever.

And now I knew, at last, why he'd seemed so familiar that first time I saw him. I hadn't recognized him then, but I did now.

I recognized him very well. Perhaps for the first time in my life.

He hadn't been dangerous after all. He'd been trying to help me. I'd just been too stubborn to see it.

I want to talk to him. I want to try to talk some sense to him, tell him the way things are.

One eye open, I watched the young man step up onto the path that led past where I lay and around to the underground garage entrance.

So heedless, so angry.

So sure of himself.

My mouth felt as dry as parchment. I didn't know if I'd be able to get out any words at all, or if I did, whether he'd hear them. Or even exactly what I'd say.

But I had to try.

Don't we all?

As the young man approached, I looked up at the sky.

Dead center in my field of vision, a lone passenger jet made its way across the clear blue vault of heaven. I wondered where it was headed. Then sent a silent prayer to help it on its course.

The young man was nearly here.

I pressed my back to the wall, uncrossed a single leg—not both—and stretched it out in front of me.

And waited.

18. THE VAGRANT

The day started out so well. Everything was going my way. Imagine my surprise when I got to the seventh floor, walked into my boss's office, and found myself summarily given the boot!

I took a side door out of the building to avoid being seen. Heading around a back corner toward the entrance to the underground garage, I didn't notice the homeless guy lying there in the shadows, his back to the wall, one leg outstretched like a stick of driftwood.

I was about to plow right into him when—

"Wait..."

It was the voice that stopped me.

I pulled up short and saw him then, sprawled out by the side of the walkway.

He wore a dirty green wool hat and one of those orange DayGlo construction vests, most of the Glo long worn off. Gloves with the fingers cut off. How old was he? Hard to say. In his fifties, I guessed, or maybe he was only a few years older than me, just in terrible shape.

"Wait," he said again. He mumbled a few more words, but all I could make out was ". . . help . . ."

Balancing my file box on my hip and holding it there with one hand, I started going for my wallet with the other. "For cryin' out loud," I grumbled. "If you have to panhandle, go do it around the front—"

"Wait," he said for the third time, and he stretched out one faltering hand. "Please."

I stopped digging for my wallet. I didn't know why, but there was something in his tone.

He started coughing, then tried to talk through his coughing fit. ". . . look . . . could use . . . a friend . . ."

Oh, yeah. I could see that, all right. This guy could use a friend, a bath, a hot meal, and a new career plan. He looked like he'd lost just about everything a person could lose.

It took a good five seconds before the penny dropped.

He wasn't talking about himself. He was saying *I* was the one who looked like I could use a friend.

Me!

Which sort of ticked me off. Hey, I had *plenty* of friends!

"Great," I said. "Whatever."

I hefted my file box with both hands, turned on my heel, and headed for the underground garage, fuming. For some reason his inane ramblings had gotten under my skin. "Shake it off, Barab," I muttered.

But I couldn't.

There was something about his voice.

Halfway to the garage I stopped. And before I knew what I was doing, I'd turned around and started walking back out to where the homeless guy lay.

"Hey," I said. "I want a word with you."

He mumbled something that sounded like ". . . ego . . . in perspective . . ."

"What? Speak up, man!"

He started to speak again but collapsed in another fit of coughing. I waited to see what he had to say, but the hacking kept going. Worse this time than before.

My irritation turned to alarm.

This guy was not okay.

I set my precious file box down and leaned over

him. "Listen, man, are you okay?" Stupid question. The guy was as far from okay as a person could get.

I straightened up and looked around, hoping to see someone, anyone, rushing over to help. Maybe someone from the hospital.

No one came.

It was just the vagrant, coughing his lungs out, and me.

"Oh, geez," I muttered.

I slid my file box over against the wall, where I prayed it would be safe for a few minutes, then got both hands under the man's arms and hoisted him to his feet. I half walked, half dragged him to the ER entrance. Got him checked in, which took forever. Then made a mad dash back out and around to the side of the building, hoping like fury that no one had come along and lifted my stuff in the few minutes I'd left it alone.

My whole life was in that box.

I rounded the corner, reached the spot where I'd left it—and stopped.

Breathed a sigh of relief.

It was still there.

I picked up the box and started for the underground garage.

Halfway there, I paused once again.

Don't stop, I told myself. *Just go get in your car and go home. This is not your concern.*

But really, what was my hurry? I'd just been fired. It wasn't even noon yet. It wasn't like I had somewhere else I had to be. At that moment, all I had to look forward to was a date with myself in my apartment, nursing a drink and a handful of grudges.

It couldn't hurt to spend a few minutes in the waiting room. See how things turned out for the old guy.

I made my way back to the ER, file box and all. I left my name at the desk and told the receptionist I was going to stay for a bit to see how John Doe was doing. He told me to take a seat and said he'd let me know.

The way he said it, I had a feeling it was touch and go.

So I took a seat. And thought about the homeless man.

What chain of events and circumstances had led him to this point in his life? I couldn't begin to imagine.

Hours went by. Finally a young woman came out and called my name.

"We're so sorry, Mr. Barab. Your friend has passed."

"He's not my—" I started to tell her he wasn't my

friend, that I'd never seen the guy before, but the words died in my throat.

In fact, I didn't say a thing. I couldn't speak.

I could hardly breathe.

Which kind of surprised me. The fact that the old man hadn't pulled through did not come as all that much of a shock. To be honest, I was kind of expecting it.

What surprised me was my own reaction.

For some reason I couldn't fathom, the vagrant's passing moved me deeply. Way more than I'd imagined it would.

The only words I'd actually heard him speak had made no sense at all.

Wait . . . help . . .

Please.

I'd dismissed it all as the ramblings of delirium, which no doubt was exactly what it was. Still, coughing and hacking aside, he'd sounded so . . . intent.

Like he'd had something he urgently needed to tell me.

I had taken a few steps toward the exit when the young woman at the ER desk called my name again. I turned back and looked at her.

"His things?" she said, holding out a paper bag.

His things?

I walked back over, took the paper bag, and brought it out to the waiting room, where I sat down with it, still feeling numb.

One by one, I went through the possessions I found in the bag.

A pair of shoes. A ragged old twenty-dollar bill. A crumpled slip of paper with one of crazy Merl's Bible verses printed on it. Ecclesiastes 1:2. I knew that one. Vanity of vanities, and so on.

I turned the slip over and found some handwriting on the back. A few words, scrawled on the top in a felt-tip pen: the date, a few weeks from now.

And a name.

I felt chills shiver up my spine.

It was *my* name.

And below that, a single hand-printed word:

Humility

I thought about that as I carried it all back to the underground garage, thought about it as I placed my file box on the passenger seat of my Toyota—my race-car—and drove out of the garage.

The whole way back to my apartment, I thought about that little slip of paper. About what it said, what it meant, and how it could have possibly ended up in my hand. About why my name was on it, and what it had to do with me.

I thought about it all that night, and all the next day, and the day after that.

I still think about it every day.

REFLECTIONS

HOW TO AVOID STUMBLING OVER YOURSELF

Y ou are talented. You have developed useful skill sets. I wish that were enough to protect you from stumbling over yourself the way Bob did. But it isn't. Bob's story is a sober warning for all leaders that talents and skills are not enough.

Bob was talented, skilled, and driven, but the big three don't guarantee success.

The following exercises and practices will help you avoid stumbling over yourself. These practices are simple and disarming. They will help you learn to set aside your defenses, at least momentarily. In those moments, you will wipe steam from the mirror and catch a glimpse of yourself in new ways.

Bob, in his naïve confidence, rejected these practices, thus incurring unnecessary self-inflicted pain and bitter experiences. Consequently, Bob's transformation was slow and painful. Your journey doesn't have to be like that. The following practices give legs to ideas that will change the way you think about yourself, others, and your world.

Everything changes when we change the way we think about ourselves. Our deepest satisfactions emerge from contribution. Self-development enhances our ability to contribute.

Become your best self.

All self-development begins with self-awareness. You must know, for example, that you can't spell before you can learn to spell.

Become self-aware.

1. Know and linger in the things that make your soul come alive.
2. Know what you don't do well but would like to do better.
3. Respect your impact on others.

The path to self-awareness hinges on the quality of your self-reflection practice.

Dan was raised on a dairy farm in central Maine and says, "I confess that, to me, discussion of things like self-awareness and self-reflection at first sounded like hippie talk. Gradually, sometimes reluctantly, I've come to see that what I thought was silliness is essential."

And there's evidence to answer the skeptics. Customer service agents who spent fifteen minutes at the end of the day reflecting about lessons learned performed 23 percent better after ten days than those who did not reflect.*

Here are five simple self-reflection projects that will change how you are in the world.

PROJECT ONE

Reflect on Bob's talents and strengths.

What did Bob do well? How was his mirror foggy? How was he self-deceived? How might your mirror be foggy?

People stumble over themselves for many reasons. As happened with Bob, your talents and strengths are a potential source of self-deception. The talents and

---

* Giada Di Stefano, Francesca Gino, Gary P. Pisano, and Bradley R. Staats, "Making Experience Count: The Role of Reflection in Individual Learning," Harvard Business School NOM Unit Working Paper No. 14-093 (June 30, 2021), SSRN, http://dx .doi.org/10.2139/ssrn.2414478

strengths you have can deceive you when you lack self-awareness. Talents and strengths you think you have, *but don't*, also deceive you. Self-deception blocks your most meaningful contribution.

Take project one to the next level by reading Bob's story with some friends. Discuss how Bob's talents and strengths caused him to stumble.

PROJECT TWO

Make a long list of your talents, strengths, skills, and aptitudes.

These are things that make your eyes go bright. Gallup defines talents as "recurring patterns of thought, feeling, or behavior that can be productively applied."* You were born with talent. A talent is something that comes to you naturally. Gallup states that strengths, on the other hand, are "the ability to provide near-perfect performance in a specific activity."†

---

* "What Is the Difference Between a Talent and a Strength?," CliftonStrengths for Students, Gallup, accessed January 18, 2022, https://towson.gallup.com/help/general/273908/difference-talent-strength.aspx

† "What Is the Difference Between a Talent and a Strength?"

Recognize and respect your talents. Develop your strengths. A person who is self-aware knows their talents and strengths.

Don't worry about getting your list of talents, strengths, skills, and aptitudes exactly right. You'll modify it as time passes. Set aside a few minutes and begin your list. Revisit the list at least once a day for the next five days.

You might challenge yourself to reflect on the contributions you currently make when you bring your best self to your family, friends, and colleagues. What contributions do these abilities and aptitudes enable you to make? What contributions do you aspire to make based on these qualities and behaviors?

Take project two to the next level by showing it to a trusted friend. Explain that you're learning to practice self-reflection to elevate your self-awareness. Ask your friend to identify your top two or three talents or strengths. You might include the following questions:

1. What am I doing when I'm at my best?
2. What is my greatest contribution to our business, family, or relationship?
3. If you were forced to choose two or three qualities or behaviors on the list that I might

improve, which would you choose? In what ways might I enhance my contribution?

Note: You may have included some *aspirational* talents and strengths on your list, that is, things you wish you were good at, or think you should be good at. You may find rich opportunities for self-development if you courageously open this window of conversation.

PROJECT THREE
Consider your impact on the people around you.

Bob stumbled over himself because he had distorted assumptions about other people's perceptions and responses. He thought he had deep relationships, but they were shallow. He thought people were trustworthy, but at least one was a backstabber. He made adversaries of people who wanted to help him.

Step One

Make a list of the people with whom you most frequently interact. With each specific person in mind, ask yourself these questions:

1. How does this person respond to me when I think I'm at my best?
2. What am I doing when this person's response to me is surprise, disappointment, or joy?

Create the following sentence for each person on your list:

[Mary] thinks I'm really good at

_____.

If you can, complete the sentence with three things. If you want to stretch yourself, include the word "admire."

[Mary] admires my ability to

_____.

Don't show your sentences to anyone. This is just for you.

Step Two

Go to the people on your list and ask them to tell you what they think you are good at. In private, compare your list to theirs. What do you observe? If you find discrepancies, perhaps it's time to wipe the fog from your mirror. If you see consistencies, how can you better use your positive qualities and behaviors to maximize your contribution to others?

Step Three

Complete the following sentence for each person on your list. If you can, complete the sentence with two or more items:

> If [Mary] revealed a way that I'm holding myself back, she would say
>
> _____.

You know what's next. Go to each person on your list and ask them how you might be holding yourself back. If you're feeling brave, ask them for specific behaviors you could practice that would propel you forward.

Next Level

Include one or two of the people on your list in your self-development process. Declare your commitment to try a new behavior. Ask if they would be willing to give you feedback in a week or two. When they give you feedback, explore ways to improve. Keep in mind, this is self-development with a purpose. How does improving increase your contribution?

PROJECT FOUR
Include others in your process.

Use the list of people you made for project three to record the top three talents, skills, or strengths of each person on your team. What do you admire about them? How might you help them move toward their best selves?

People who learn to help others can learn to help themselves if they practice self-reflection. How would you like to help others maximize their talent? How would you help people avoid stumbling over themselves? How might this outward perspective expand your thinking about yourself?

Expand your approach.

It's dangerous to walk the path of self-discovery alone.

You might think self-reflection and self-awareness are best practiced in isolation. If you think that, you're being Bob. We see ourselves more clearly when we include others in the process. When we don't, when we reflect purely on our own, apart from others, the problem of self-deception is inevitable. You may not be as out of touch as Bob, but you're still confused if you don't see yourself through others' eyes.

PROJECT FIVE
Reflect on the problems you face.

Life is filled with problems. Some people like to call them "challenges," but for this exercise I'm using the term "problems," nasty nagging issues that tend to beat you down and make you feel weak.

Problems contain within them the potential of personal transformation. Problems always change you. They sometimes narrow your focus and solidify your existing outlook. But, if you leverage them, the world grows wider, and you develop openness.

Problems change the way you think about yourself, others, and the world. Bob's problems inspired fear, frustration, and blame. Self-reflection could have taken Bob in an upward trajectory, if he'd let it.

The following self-reflection is designed to help you get the most out of problems. Please don't think of it as a problem-solving strategy. It's a strategy for growing through problems.

Bring a problem to mind, something that tightens your stomach. That pit in your stomach is responsibility. If you didn't feel responsible, you wouldn't care.

1. List the aspects of this situation that are within your control.
2. What uncomfortable truths—about yourself—come to mind when you reflect on this problem?
3. Who comes to mind when you tell yourself, *I might want to talk with* ... ?
4. Who or what are you blaming for this problem? How is blame helping you? Harming you?
5. Imagine this problem had good intentions and a voice: Who is this problem calling you to become?

Four reminders:

1. Problems remind us we aren't the center of the universe.
2. Problems make us hungry.

3. The strongest approach to a problem is curiosity.
4. "Why me?" thinking is the voice of entitle-
   ment.

The final application of this self-reflection is listing the behaviors and attitudes that serve you while grappling with this problem.

FINAL THOUGHTS

Looking inward to reflect is necessary for self-awareness and growth. But constantly thinking about yourself is like pouring poison in your own well.

Here is the difference between self-reflection and self-absorption: the former is liberating; the latter imprisons by creating self-inflicted anxiety.

Self-reflection:

1. Reveals who you are.
2. Empowers healthy decision-making.
3. Exposes negative patterns before they become destructive habits.
4. Enables useful service.
5. Maximizes joyful contribution.
6. Enables you to escape unhealthy navel-gazing.

The purpose of self-reflection is to expand your capacity to serve.

Self-absorption:

1. Replaces self-reflection by focusing on what's happening to you.
2. Weakens decision-making skills.
3. Reinforces negative patterns until they become destructive habits.
4. Undermines ability to perform useful service.
5. Prevents joyful contribution.

You stumble over yourself when you believe you're the center of the universe. A person absorbed with themself feels frustrated and offended when you don't focus on them. Healthy leaders think, *"It's all about others."*

Turn inward so you can turn outward. Turning inward is a means to an end, not an end in itself.

Self-reflection makes growth possible and contribution meaningful.

QUESTIONS FOR REFLECTION AND DISCUSSION

1. The book opens with quotes from *The Shawshank Redemption*, the book of Job, and Warren Bennis's *On Becoming a Leader*. Why do you think the authors chose these three particular passages? What do they have to say about the story? What meaning do they hold for you?

2. What do you think happens next, after the end of chapter eighteen? How do you think the next few days and weeks might play out for this version of Bob? Why?

3. How are the events of the final chapter different from the events of the first chapter? What specifically do you think causes those differences?

4. How is the Bob of chapters fifteen and sixteen different from the Bob of the story's opening? What

has changed in his character and personality, and why do you think that happens? What specific examples can you find of how his behavior shifts over the last few chapters, say, in chapters thirteen through seventeen?

5. What specific moments or events in the story can you pinpoint that cause a significant shift in Bob's perspective, attitude, or behavior? Have there been similar key shift moments in your life? How have they affected you, and why?

6. When the other people in the shelter call Bob "Bobby," it doesn't bother him, although in earlier years it would have driven him nuts. And when Anne takes to calling him "Robert," he finds he actually likes it. Why now, and why not before?

7. Most of the relationships Bob has with other people in the story turn out to be quite different from how he initially sees them. What examples of this can you point out? How does he at first misread each of these people, and why?

8. Did you notice moments when Bob defended himself? It might be interesting to go through the story and note every time he does so. Why do you suppose he does this? Does he stop doing it at any point, and if so, when?

9. Did you notice how Bob tends to use the phrase "to be honest…"? How does it make you feel when people frequently use phrases like "to be honest," or "to tell you the truth," or "trust me"?

10. In the opening of the book, Bob recounts how he didn't recognize the man he tripped over, and then says, "I still wonder how things would have turned out if I had." Have there been key moments in your life when you've wondered something similar—how things might have gone differently if you'd seen something you missed? Take a moment right now to identify two or three specific times this has happened to you. What can you learn from those moments, and how can you apply that insight going forward in your life?

11. From the very first paragraph, *The Vagrant* is in many ways all about Bob's blind spots. It takes the mirror of honest people around him, like Gavin, Lacy, and Lucius, for him to finally start seeing himself as others do. (One pivotal scene of recognition takes place as he looks in an actual mirror.) In what ways might your inner mirror be blurry? Do you have any blind spots in your own ability to see yourself? If you do, what are they?

12. In chapter eight, Bob's dad says that if he could talk to his twenty-year-old self, he would say, "More compassion. Less certainty." What do you think he means by that?

13. Bob's file box contains what he calls his "most prized possessions." Why do you suppose he's been keeping these things in his office? What do they mean? If Bob were to compile a file box at the end of chapter sixteen, after his months at the shelter, what do you think he would put in it? What would you put in your file box?

14. Included in Bob's file box are three books that are meaningful to him. Later, at the shelter, he picks out a new set of three books. How are these two trios of books different? What does each book mean to Bob, and what does that say about him? If you had to choose three books to go into your "precious file box," what would they be? Why did you select those three?

15. The "impediments of the apocalypse" the homeless man speaks of in chapter one seem to be an oblique reference to the "four horsemen of the apocalypse" referred to in several books of the Christian Bible, traditionally viewed as punishments sent by God. Why do you think the man

uses the word "impediments" here? What does he mean by "apocalypse"? And what about that odd comment he adds: "They fly on wings of gold, but it's an illusion"?

16. The authors added the subtitle "The Inner Journey of Leadership." What does this story say to you about leadership?

17. Bob's boss Norman, the Coach, Uncle Bill, Anne at the shelter, and Bob himself all occupy types of leadership positions. How is each one's approach to leadership different?

18. There is one character in the story who never utters a word, yet in some ways his presence is pivotal. Why do you think the authors chose the name "Merlin" for this character? And what does he represent to you?

19. What do you feel are the two or three most significant lessons the story illustrates? How and why are these important to you?

20. Bob describes himself as feeling "humiliated" a number of times in the story. We've all had experiences where we felt humiliated. Take a moment to identify two or three such times in your life. Did those experiences change you in any way, and if so, how?

21. In ornithology, as Anne explains, the term "vagrant" refers to a bird that has strayed from or been blown off its path. Has there ever been a time in your life when that description might have applied to you?

Acknowledgments

E very book starts with an idea scribbled in the boat-builder's tent, then sets off on a long trail of left turns and false starts, of thoughts tried and discarded, then recaptured and tested again, all marked by tens of thousands of scratches on paper, until a vaguely finished rough draft staggers down to the pier to be pushed out into the harbor and water-tested.

Which is when all the magnificent people of the shore crew show up and start going over the thing from top to bottom, helping to make the thing shipshape and keep us from drowning before we even reach the open sea on our voyage.

The authors send up a hearty thank-you:

To Glenn Yeffeth, captain of the good ship Ben-Bella, for believing in our little story; Gregory Newton Brown, for his deftly sensitive editorial hand; Sarah Avinger, for the exquisite jacket design; and the rest of our expert team at BenBella Books: Kim Broderick, Jennifer Canzoneri, Jennifer Greenstein, Alicia Kania, Adrienne Lang, Monica Lowry, Rachel Phares, and Leah Wilson.

To our eagle-eyed early readers: Faye Atchison, Deb and Charlie Austin, Dan Clements, Bill Ellis, Phil Gerbyshak, James Justice, Adrian Mann, Margret McBride, Abbie McClung, Dondi Scumaci, who helped us make this a better book.

To Mollie Marti, J.D., PhD, for her perspective on legal questions surrounding Bob Barab's abrupt dismissal from Mercy Hospital.

To Reverend John Ineson, for the joke about the guy who lost his Rolex; and the quirkily brilliant Steven Wright, for the joke about the guy who goes to the bookstore.

To the legions of loyal followers of the *Leadership Freak* blog over the years.

And finally to you, faithful reader and fellow voyagers on this ocean of self-discovery. We hope *The Vagrant* serves you well and brings you joy.

About the Authors

Dan Rockwell (leadershipfreak.blog) gave his first presentation at the age of sixteen and has been delivering presentations and workshops ever since. Dan's fascination with leadership led him to launch his *Leadership Freak* blog in January 2010. Today *Leadership Freak* is read in virtually every country on the globe, with nearly five hundred thousand subscribers to its various social media channels. Dan has been named among the "Top 50 Leadership and Management Experts" and "Top 100 Leadership Speakers" by *Inc.* magazine and the "Top 30 Leaders in Business of 2014" by the American Management Association. His blog has been hailed as the "most socially shared leadership blog on the internet" by the Center for Management and Organization Effectiveness.

In addition to gaining a devoted online following,

the blog opened up numerous opportunities to deliver keynotes and workshops. Dan's extensive client list includes Chick-fil-A Supply, the National Institutes of Health, Ace Hardware, the National Association of Federally-Insured Credit Unions, Home Depot, Ducks Unlimited, Ascension Health, the Florida Department of Transportation, Geisinger Health System, the Illinois Association of School Administrators, LexisNexis, Allegra Network, Homeland Security, the US Department of the Navy, the Washington State Department of Transportation, the World Leaders Conference West Palm Beach, The Institute for Public Procurement, Cable One, Inc., and Royal Caribbean International.

Dan holds an MBA and undergraduate degrees in theology, pastoral ministry, and construction and design. He has owned two businesses and serves in church ministry. Dan spent fifteen years as a workforce development consultant for a Penn State University special affiliate, in which capacity he designed courses, hired and mentored instructors, and delivered hundreds of presentations for local, regional, and global organizations. He currently coaches leaders, consults with organizations, and delivers corporate and community presentations around the country.

Dan lives in central Pennsylvania with his wife of forty-seven years.

John David Mann (johndavidmann.com) is an award-winning author whose accolades include the Nautilus Award, the Axiom Business Book Award (Gold Medal), BookPal's Outstanding Works of Literature (OWL) Award, and the 2017 Living Now Book Awards' Evergreen Medal, given for his "contribution to positive global change." His books have been cited in *Inc.*'s "Most Motivational Books Ever Written," HubSpot's "20 Most Highly Rated Sales Books of All Time," *Entrepreneur*'s "10 Books Every Leader Should Read," *Forbes*'s "8 Books Every Young Leader Should Read," CNBC's "10 Books That Boost Money IQ," and NPR's "Great Reads," and have included a *Financial Times*'s "Book of the Month" club selection.

John's books have been published in three dozen languages and have sold more than three million copies. In addition to coauthoring the bestselling Go-Giver series with Bob Burg, which has sold over one million copies, he is the coauthor of the *New York Times* bestsellers *The Latte Factor* (with David Bach), *The Red Circle* (with Brandon Webb), and *Flash Foresight* (with Daniel Burrus), and the national bestsellers *Out of the Maze* (with Spencer Johnson), *Among Heroes* (with Brandon Webb), *The Slight Edge* (with Jeff Olson), and *Real Leadership* (with John Addison). His *Take the Lead* (with Betsy Myers) was named Best

Leadership Book of 2011 by Tom Peters and the *Washington Post*.

His first novel, *Steel Fear* (coauthored with Brandon Webb), was hailed by Lee Child as "an instant classic, maybe an instant legend," singled out by *Publishers Weekly* as one of the "Best Books of 2021," and nominated for a Barry Award.

John is married to Ana Gabriel Mann, his coauthor on *The Go-Giver Marriage*, and considers himself the luckiest mann in the world.